CAMBODIA'S ECONOMIC DIVERSIFICATION

A COUNTRY DIAGNOSTIC STUDY

NOVEMBER 2024

ASIAN DEVELOPMENT BANK

6 ADB Avenue, Mandaluyong City, 1550 Metro Manila, Philippines
Tel +63 2 8632 4444; Fax +63 2 8636 2444
www.adb.org

ISBN 978-92-9270-971-6 (print); 978-92-9270-972-3 (PDF); 978-92-9270-973-0 (ebook)
Publication Stock No. TCS240493-2
DOI: http://dx.doi.org/10.22617/TCS240493-2

Corrigenda to ADB publications may be found at http://www.adb.org/publications/corrigenda.

Notes:
In this publication, "$" refers to United States dollars and "KR" refers to riel.
ADB recognizes "China" as the People's Republic of China, "Korea" as the Republic of Korea, "Laos" as the Lao People's Democratic Republic, "Republic of Turkey" as Türkiye, and "United States of America" as the United States.

Cover design by Joe Mark Ganaban.

Contents

Tables, Figures, and Box

Tables

Figures

Box

Acknowledgments

This report was prepared with support from the Asian Development Bank (ADB) technical assistance project, 6811: Economic Diagnostic Studies in Asia and the Pacific (Subproject 1), to help the Government of Cambodia develop policies and strategies for economic diversification and improve global competitiveness.

A team of ADB staff and consultants produced this report. Sophie Nguyen and consultant Jayant Menon headed the ADB team, with Maria Rowena Cham and Socheatda Nem providing support. Lei Lei Song, director of the Economic Analysis and Operational Support Division, provided overall guidance for the study.

Special thanks to the staff of the Cambodia Resident Mission and the peer reviewers from ADB departments who provided information and valuable suggestions, coordinated field missions, and participated in the review of the study.

The team appreciates the helpful input made by the Government of Cambodia, its agencies, industry associations, and the firms that were interviewed for this study.

Peter Fredenburg was the economics editor, and Tuesday Soriano was the copy editor. Joe Mark Ganaban did the graphic design, layout, and typesetting. Bhabhani Dewan and Rene Cris Rivera assisted with proofreading and administrative tasks.

Abbreviations

ADB	–	Asian Development Bank
ASEAN	–	Association of Southeast Asian Nations
CDS	–	country diagnostic study
COVID-19	–	coronavirus disease
PRC	–	People's Republic of China
ECI	–	economic complexity index
FDI	–	foreign direct investment
FTA	–	free trade agreement
GDP	–	gross domestic product
GFC	–	global financial crisis
LDC	–	least-developed country
M2	–	broad money that includes cash and highly liquid accounts
MFI	–	microfinance institution
MFN	–	most favored nation
MoP	–	margin of preference
MSMEs	–	micro, small, and medium-sized enterprises
NBC	–	National Bank of Cambodia
OECD	–	Organisation for Economic Co-operation and Development
QIP	–	qualified investment project
RCA	–	revealed comparative advantage

Currency Equivalents

(as of 11 December 2023)

Currency unit	–	**Riel**
KR0.00	=	$0.000
$1.00	=	KR000.00

1 Introduction

Overview and Context

Cambodia has undergone a profound transition from a planned to a market economy in the past 4 decades. Cambodia began to embrace market-oriented reforms in the late 1980s. In 1987, the government abolished the state monopoly on foreign trade and 2 years later opened up trade to the private sector when it promulgated a liberal foreign investment code. While the results of these early economic reforms were somewhat lackluster, progress on the political front in the 1990s accelerated economic reform as the government implemented wide-ranging measures to liberalize trade and investment. Reforms gained further momentum after Cambodia joined the Association of Southeast Asian Nations (ASEAN) in 1999.

Since joining ASEAN, Cambodia's gross domestic product (GDP) has grown by an average of more than 7% per year, making the country one of the fastest-growing economies in Asia and the world. In 2024, Cambodia became the first least-developed country (LDC) to join the World Trade Organization. In the same year, the government adopted its Rectangular Strategy for Growth, Employment, Equity, and Efficiency to guide Cambodia's development objectives and strategies. The Rectangular Strategy has gone through several iterations, each building on the successes of previous versions and learning from shortcomings. The focus has always been on promoting economic growth, reducing poverty, and ensuring equitable and sustainable development.

The previous country diagnostic study (CDS) for Cambodia was conducted about a decade ago and published in 2014 (ADB 2014). Much has happened in this decade. While significant economic and social progress was made until 2019, the coronavirus disease (COVID-19) pandemic, which lasted from 2020 to 2022, dealt a devastating blow to the country. Partly for this reason, many of the challenges identified in the earlier CDS are still binding constraints today.

The previous CDS stated that Cambodia needed to redouble its efforts to promote economic diversification and upgrade its industry while continuing to leverage its comparative advantages (ADB 2014). This observation remains as true today as it was a decade ago. The critical constraints on inclusive growth identified then included deficits in human capital, infrastructure, governance, and the national savings rate. These broad categories of constraints also included the high cost of electricity, macroeconomic risks, inadequate access to finance, and many types of market failure. All of these constraints are still present today, although some are less binding than they were a decade ago. In the meantime, new challenges have emerged, some unrelated to the pandemic.

This study updates the previous CDS and examines what remains to be done for Cambodia to achieve its goal of becoming an upper middle-income country by 2030. In addition to highlighting the need to continue working to overcome long-standing constraints, this CDS analyzes emerging challenges and how they can be addressed. As in previous CDSs, the focus is on overcoming constraints on inclusive growth, particularly impediments to greater economic diversification. This is consistent with the objectives of the Government of Cambodia as stated in its various long-term strategic plans, including the previous Rectangular Strategy (Phase IV), 2018–2023 and the current Pentagon Strategy (Phase I).

The Rectangular Strategy (Phase IV) targeted annual GDP growth at 7%. It sought to reduce the poverty rate to below 10% by 2023—which might have happened without the pandemic. It further aimed to transform Cambodia into an upper middle-income country by 2030, a challenging target that is still being pursued. It identified four priority areas for reform: (i) human resources development, (ii) economic diversification, (iii) promotion of private sector development and employment, and (iv) inclusive and sustainable development.

The government's current Pentagon Strategy (Phase I) seeks to ensure that Cambodia realizes its aspiration to become an upper middle-income country by 2030 and a high-income country by 2050. It retains the four priority areas of the Rectangular Strategy, but adds another on sustainability and resilience, particularly targeting the digital economy.

Sustained policy reforms have helped Cambodia make significant economic progress. The economy more than doubled in nominal terms from $12 billion in 2010 to $27 billion in 2019, just before the pandemic hit. Real GDP grew by an average of 7% over the same period, with increased integration into the global economy a hallmark of this growth. The share of Cambodia's trade in GDP rose from 93% in 2010 to 132% in 2019, much higher than the average of 48% in Asia and the Pacific (Karamba, Tong, and Salcher 2022). This share increased further to 180% in 2021. Real gross national income per capita doubled from $750 in 2010 to $1,560 in 2019, lifting Cambodia to lower middle-income status in 2015 (Table 1). Gross national income hovered during the pandemic at $1,580 in 2021 and then increased again to $1,690 in 2022.

The economy has weathered several regional and global shocks, most notably the Asian financial crisis of 1997–1998, the global financial crisis (GFC) of 2008–2009, and, most recently, the COVID-19 pandemic. The Asian financial crisis had little impact on Cambodia because the country was not yet strongly integrated into the region. However, when the GFC hit, Cambodia suffered one of the largest growth contractions in ASEAN because of its heavy reliance on the United States (US) as an export market (Menon 2022a). The pandemic also dealt Cambodia a huge blow, reversing hard-won gains in human development (Table 1). However, the economy is now on the mend and its medium-term prospects are favorable. Nevertheless, long-standing challenges remain, and some new ones have emerged. Cambodia will need to accelerate its reform efforts to achieve its goal of becoming an upper middle-income country by 2030.

Table 1: Selected Macroeconomic Indicators

Indicator	2010	2011	2012	2013	2014	2015	2016	2017	2018	2019	2020	2021	2022	2023
Real GDP growth (%)	6.0	7.1	7.3	7.5	7.1	7.0	7.0	6.9	7.5	7.1	(3.1)	3.0	5.2	5.5
GDP per capita ($)	830	911	971	1,057	1,136	1,218	1,330	1,429	1,555	1,694	1,606	1,648	1,800	1,942
Nominal GDP ($ billon)	12	13	14	15	17	18	20	22	24	27	26	27	30	33
Consumer price inflation (period average, %)	4.0	5.5	2.9	2.9	3.9	1.2	3.0	2.9	2.5	1.9	2.9	2.9	5.3	3.0
Nominal exchange rate (KR/$, period average)	4,044	4,016	4,033	4,027	4,030	4,025	4,030	4,048	4,065	4,070	4,078	4,095	4,090	4,065
Trade (% of GDP)	93.3	100.3	106.1	121.3	102.6	109.5	114.8	117.6	125.5	132.6	149.3	180.1	...	...
Current account balance (% of GDP)	(8.4)	(7.9)	(8.6)	(8.4)	(8.6)	(8.8)	(8.6)	(8.1)	(11.8)	(15.0)	(8.5)	(45.7)	(29.0)	(17.6)
Fiscal balance (% of GDP)	(9.8)	(9.0)	(8.8)	(8.8)	(7.9)	(0.6)	(0.3)	(0.8)	0.7	3.0	(3.4)	(7.1)	(5.5)	(3.6)

... = data not available, ( ) = negative, GDP = gross domestic product.
Source: Asian Development Bank estimates.

2 Recent Economic Developments

Growth and Macroeconomic Performance

Economic growth. Cambodia was from 2000 to 2019 one of fastest-growing economies in Southeast Asia, with an average growth rate of 7.6% per year. The country was significantly affected by the GFC, which slowed real GDP growth to only 0.1% in 2009, but it recovered quickly and returned to real growth of 6.0% the following year. From 2010 until the onset of the COVID-19 pandemic in 2019, Cambodia's real GDP grew at an average rate of 7.0% (Figure 1).

Figure 1: Real GDP Growth, 2010–2023
(% year on year)

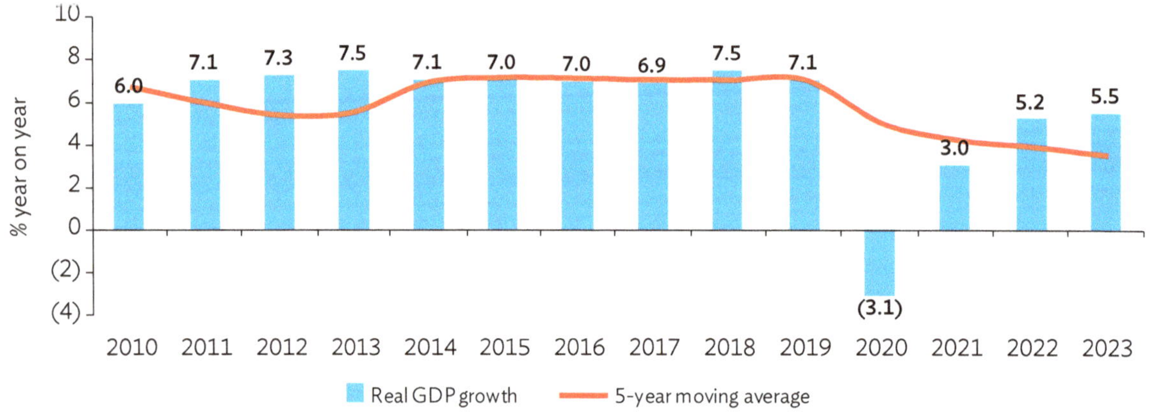

( ) = negative, GDP = gross domestic product.
Source: Asian Development Bank estimates.

Cambodia managed the COVID-19 pandemic relatively well. After a 3.1% decline in 2020, real GDP growth rebounded to 3.0% in 2021 and 5.2% in 2022, thanks in large part to effective containment and a highly successful vaccination program that allowed the country to reopen its borders in November 2021. With the highest vaccination rate in a developing country and the sixth highest in the world, Cambodia led the region in reopening.

Cambodia's economy grew by 5.2% in 2022 and 5.3% in 2023, as domestic demand recovered and higher external demand allowed growth to gradually return to pre-pandemic levels.

Supply-side drivers. Cambodia's economic trajectory has been underpinned by a fundamental transformation on the supply side, with industry and services becoming the main drivers of GDP growth (Figure 2).

Figure 2: Supply-Side Contributions to GDP Growth, 2010–2023

(% year on year)

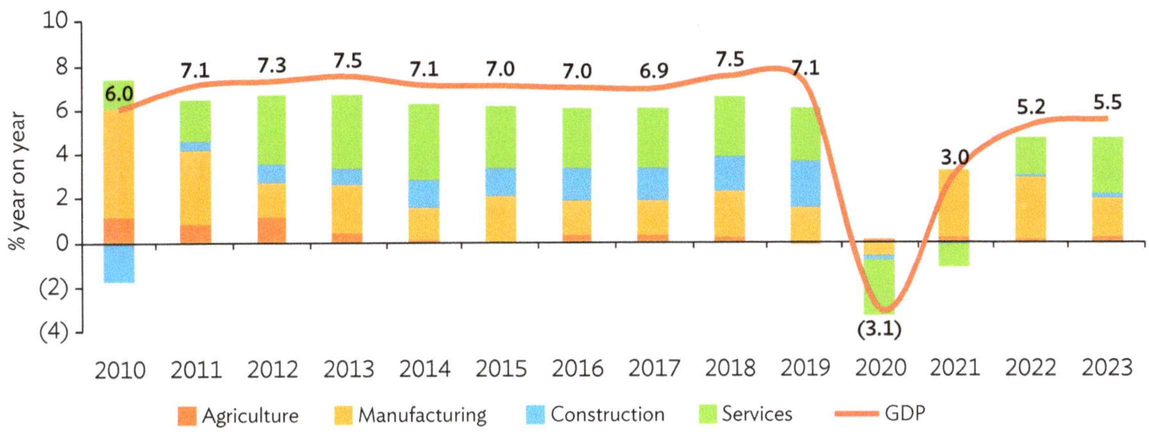

( ) = negative, GDP = gross domestic product.
Source: Asian Development Bank estimates.

Garment manufacturing has been the primary driver of growth in industry, with value added in this segment alone amounting to roughly a fourth of Cambodia's real GDP. Low labor costs, favorable investment policies, and preferential access to markets such as the US and the European Union have made Cambodia an attractive location for export-oriented garment manufacturing. Construction is the second-largest driver of growth in the industry, the building boom fueled in part by a surge in foreign investment in real estate.

The service sector has also grown rapidly in recent years as a result of the phenomenal expansion of tourism. International tourist arrivals increased from 2.5 million in 2010 to 6.6 million in 2019, and international tourism receipts accounted for an average of 26% of exports during this period. The pandemic, of course, dealt a huge blow to tourism, with arrivals plummeting to 1.3 million and receipts falling to less than 6% of exports in 2020. This dragged the share of services in GDP down from almost 40% in 2015 to 34% in 2021.

While the share of agriculture in GDP has fallen from half in the early 1990s to only a fifth, it still provides almost 40% of jobs. Agriculture is therefore important to Cambodia's economy and is likely to remain so in the foreseeable future. Cambodia's main agricultural product is rice, which is grown throughout the country and covers almost 70% of the cultivated land. Subsidiary and industrial crops grow on 19%, rubber on 7%, and permanent crops on 4% (ADB 2021). Cambodia has enormous potential for high-value agricultural exports, thanks to its abundance of arable land and favorable climate. The government has implemented policies to improve agricultural productivity, and there has been some success in recent years in diversifying agricultural exports toward higher-value products. Crops with high export potential include organic rice, cashew nuts, vegetables, and fruit (ADB 2021). Efforts to add value have focused on rice milling and strengthening agricultural value chains (Menon and Roth 2022).

Demand-side drivers. On the demand side, private consumption made the largest contribution to aggregate demand from 2010 to 2019, as rising incomes increased consumer spending on durable goods, other goods, and services. Private consumption grew at an average rate of 6.4% during this period, but contracted by 4.3% in 2020 and 3.7% in 2021 in the wake of COVID-19. To cushion the impact of the pandemic, the government significantly ramped up spending in both years, such that government consumption surged by 13% in 2020 and almost 79% in 2021. Investment in real estate has risen considerably in recent years, spurring the development of high-rise buildings, condominiums, and commercial centers in urban areas. Public investment in new infrastructure such as highways, bridges, and airports has also contributed to the growth of the construction sector and is expected to increase further. Overall, however, the contribution of investment to GDP growth remains lower than would be desirable for a country aiming for rapid growth. In addition, investment should be redirected from real estate and domestic services to the production of tradable goods (Figure 3).

Figure 3: Demand-Side Contributions to GDP Growth, 2010–2023
(% year on year)

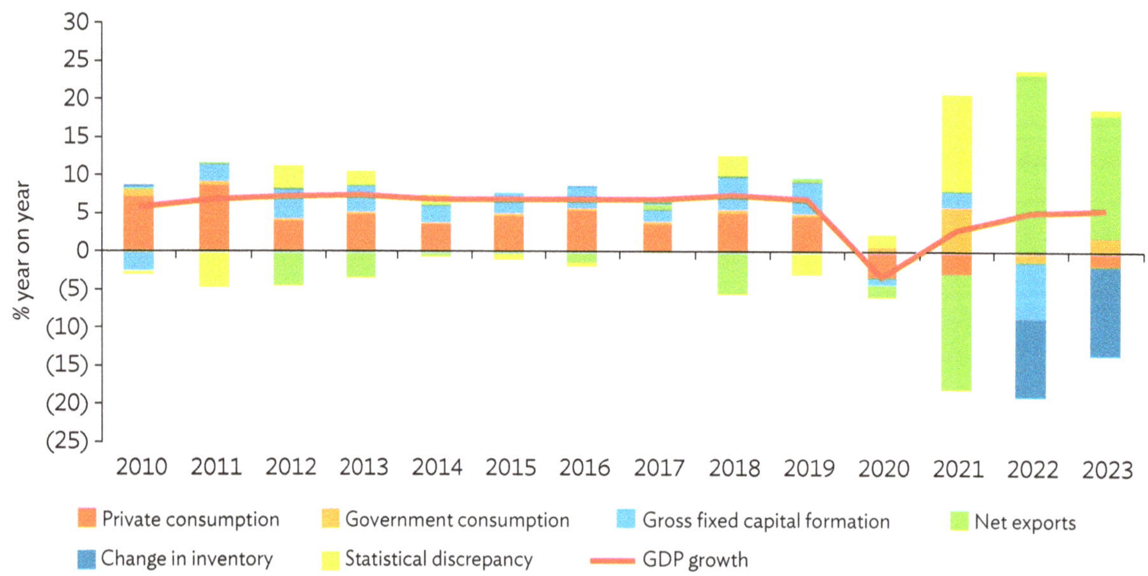

( ) = negative, GDP = gross domestic product.
Source: Asian Development Bank estimates.

Productivity drivers. Cambodia's growth story is largely one of capital accumulation, with capital contributing as much as 85% of growth in 2005–2010 and 77% in 2010–2015 (Figure 4). During these years, the contribution of labor to growth increased from 36% to 59%, while the share of total factor productivity, which measures efficiency and innovation, was negative, worsening from −22% to −36%. In 2015–2021, the contribution of capital to growth declined by almost half to 41%, but the share of labor also fell to 23%. The contribution of total factor productivity became positive in the same period, rising to 36%.

Figure 4: Contributions from Capital, Labor, and TFP to Growth, 2000–2021

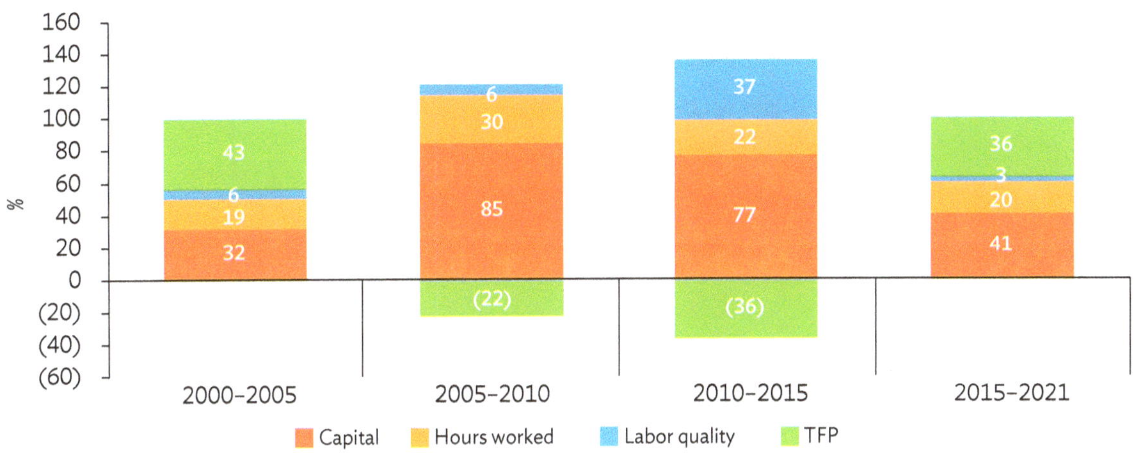

() = negative, TFP = total factor productivity.
Note: Numbers may not sum precisely because of rounding.
Source: Asian Productivity Organization. 2023. *APO Productivity Handbook 2023*. https://www.apo-tokyo.org/wp-content/uploads/2023/12/APO-Productivity-Databook-2023.pdf.

Monetary and Financial Performance

Inflation and money supply. Despite volatile import prices, exchange rate fluctuations, and external shocks such as the COVID-19 pandemic, Cambodia has enjoyed relatively low inflation and stable money supply trends over the past 2 decades. This stability comes in part from the high rate of dollarization of the economy (see below). The inflation rate in Cambodia averaged about 3% from 2011 to 2019. While inflation accelerated from 1.9% in 2019 to 2.9% in 2020 and 2021, it remained well within the government's target range of 2%–4%. Inflation then surged to 5.3% in 2022 as prices for energy, agricultural inputs, and food rose when the Russian invasion of Ukraine disrupted supply. As these effects dissipated, inflation eased to about 3% in 2023 (Figure 5).

Figure 5: Inflation, 2010–2023
(% change year on year)

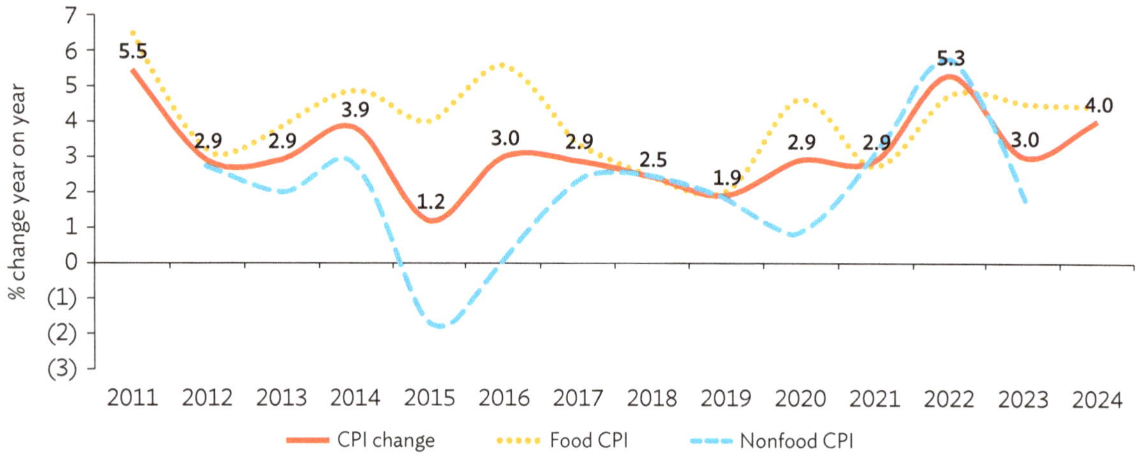

( ) = negative, CPI = consumer price index.
Source: Asian Development Bank estimates.

Broad money supply (M2) grew at an average annual rate of 23% from 2010 to 2019, reflecting the expansion of Cambodia's financial system and economic growth. Money supply growth eased to 15% in 2020 and held steady at 16% in 2021, despite the National Bank of Cambodia (NBC) pursuing an accommodative monetary policy in the wake of COVID-19.

The NBC remains committed to maintaining a stable macroeconomic environment through accommodative but disciplined monetary policy. The International Monetary Fund (IMF) Article IV consultation noted that the NBC had taken appropriate measures to support bank liquidity and thus ensure financial stability (IMF 2022).

De-dollarization. Cambodia's official currency is the Cambodian riel, but the US dollar is widely used instead. The country's dependence on the US dollar is a long-standing issue dating back to 1992–1993 and the establishment of the United Nations Transitional Authority in Cambodia, a peacekeeping operation under the 1991 Paris Peace Accords. While dollarization has stabilized prices and exchange rates, it has also rendered monetary policy ineffective and undermined the NBC's role as lender of last resort. De-dollarization is a major objective under the National Strategy for Financial Sector Development, 2016–2025.

The NBC's measures to increase the use of the riel include the mandate that financial institutions hold at least 10% of their loan portfolios in the local currency and the introduction of a liquidity-providing collateralized operation, a facility designed to help banks make more riel available to the banking system. The NBC aims to boost the use of the riel in everyday transactions by encouraging businesses to price their goods and services in riel, by calling for the development of mobile banking and electronic payments that support riel transactions, and requiring that public bills and taxes be paid in riel (Kunmakara 2023; Amarthalingam 2020).

While some of the measures implemented by the NBC increase the use of the riel as a medium of exchange, the real challenge in de-dollarizing the economy is to increase the use of the riel as a store of value. Requiring financial institutions to lend a certain portion of their portfolio in riel can only go so far. De-dollarization cannot be sustainably enforced by decree, as enforcement that significantly curtails or bans the use of dollars is likely to fail (Menon 2008). This is because dollarization is not the problem, but merely a symptom of it: a lack of confidence in the riel borne of an underdeveloped monetary system, economic vulnerability, and weak legal and institutional structures. These problems need to be addressed directly. Once they are addressed and confidence in the riel is buoyed, dollarization will naturally fade and cease to be a constraint.[1]

Finance sector. Cambodia's finance sector has grown significantly in recent years, driven by government policy, foreign investment, and a growing middle class. Nevertheless, the sector is still at an early stage of development and remains dominated by local and foreign banking institutions. There are some listed corporate bonds, and nine companies are listed on Cambodia's stock exchange.

Cambodia has seen a rapid increase in private sector credit, which accounts for 178% of GDP. Most of the credit is flowing into the real estate and construction sectors, which poses additional risks. The IMF (2022) noted that credit growth could be tamped down by several factors, such as revised prudential regulations, increased competition for funding from commercial banks, a decrease in deposit withdrawals at the NBC, and a possible decrease in collateral value and a consequent increase in nonperforming loans. The NBC believes that the banks are liquid and have sufficient capital, but there is concern that lenient regulations may allow them to exaggerate their capital and play down their nonperforming loans.

Fiscal Performance

Before the pandemic, Cambodia had a favorable fiscal balance and relatively low debt. From 2015 to 2019, the government recorded small surpluses or deficits of less than 1% of GDP, thanks to a buoyant economy and a significant increase in revenue from taxes on goods and services. A comprehensive reform of public financial management has improved budget formulation and execution, with domestic revenue mobilization nearly tripling from the equivalent of 12.6% of GDP in 2010 to 26.8% in 2019.

Then the pandemic hit Cambodia's fiscal position severely, prompting the government to implement a series of measures to support the economy, most notably a countercyclical response package worth $836 million, more than 3% of projected 2020 GDP, to address the impact of the pandemic on health, social welfare, and the economy. The social assistance program, which provided cash subsidies to impoverished and vulnerable households, received a budget of $300 million (ADB 2023a). Other government measures included partial wage subsidies for workers furloughed from the tourism,

[1] This has been the de-dollarization experience in many other dollarized economies all around the world, as summarized in Fischer (2006): "For a long time, it seemed that the extent of... dollarization was impervious to improved economic performance. Now however we have several examples of countries that have de-dollarized successfully..., including Israel, Poland, Mexico, Egypt, and Türkiye . And some signs of declining dollarization are evident in Latin American countries where it seemed that dollarization was impossible to reverse." Since then, many of the Latin American countries Fisher alludes to have successfully used market-friendly approaches to de-dollarize, including Bolivia, Paraguay, Peru, and Uruguay (García-Escribano and Sosa 2011; Cartas 2010). Cambodia would do well to heed the lessons of these countries and resist the temptation to try to enforce de-dollarization, instead continue with economic reforms that will eventually lead to sustainable de-dollarization.

garment, footwear, and textile industries; improved access to credit for small and medium-sized enterprises; and granted temporary tax exemptions to affected businesses in manufacturing, tourism, and aviation.

This expansionary stance put pressure on government finances. From a surplus of 3.0% of GDP in 2019, Cambodia's fiscal balance swung to a deficit of 2.4% in 2020 and 7.1% in 2021. Domestic revenue collection fell to 24% of GDP in 2020 and 22% in 2021. However, fiscal performance improved in 2022, with the recovery in revenue growth. The deficit in the fiscal balance decreased to 5.5% of GDP in 2022 and was expected to decline further to 3.6% in 2023 (Figure 6).

Figure 6: Fiscal Indicators, 2010–2023
(% of GDP)

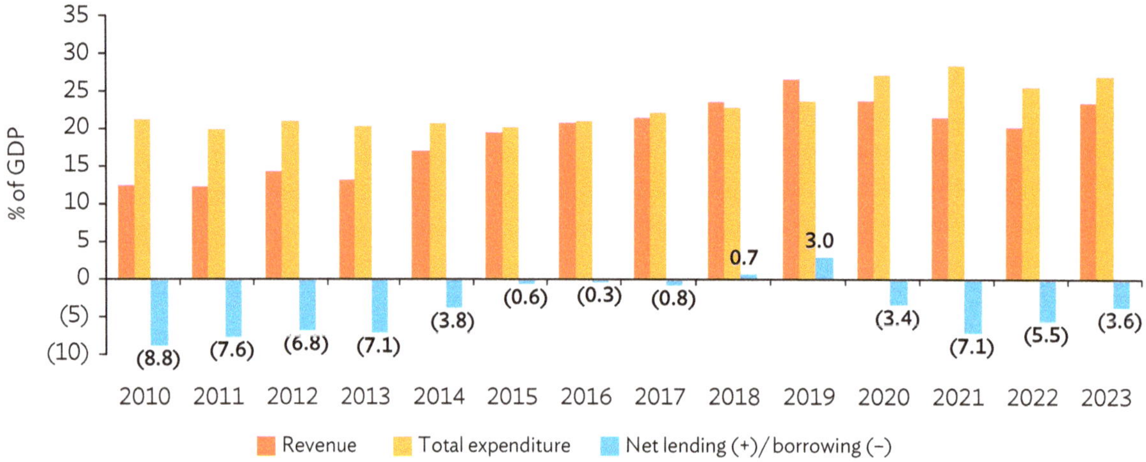

( ) = negative, GDP = gross domestic product.
Source: Asian Development Bank estimates.

The pandemic had a notable impact on Cambodia's debt. Before the pandemic, government debt amounted to roughly 30% of GDP from 2010 to 2019. In 2020 and 2021, it rose to about 35% of GDP. At the end of 2021, it was $9.5 billion, of which 42.7% was owed to the People's Republic of China (PRC). Government debt as a percentage of GDP was estimated at about 36% in 2022 and projected to rise further to 37% in 2023 (Figure 7). Despite these recent increases, debt remains at a low level for a least-developed country (LDC) like Cambodia.

The government's expansionary fiscal policy continued in 2023 as the government remains committed to prioritizing socioeconomic interventions as outlined in the Strategic Framework and Programs for Economic Recovery in the Context of Living with COVID-19 in the New Normal, 2021–2023. Nonetheless, the government is aware of the need to improve its fiscal position over the long term. Ongoing efforts to improve revenue collection and control expenditure aim to reduce the fiscal deficit in the coming years while supporting the country's development goals.

Figure 7: Government Debt, 2010–2023
(KR trillion and % of GDP)

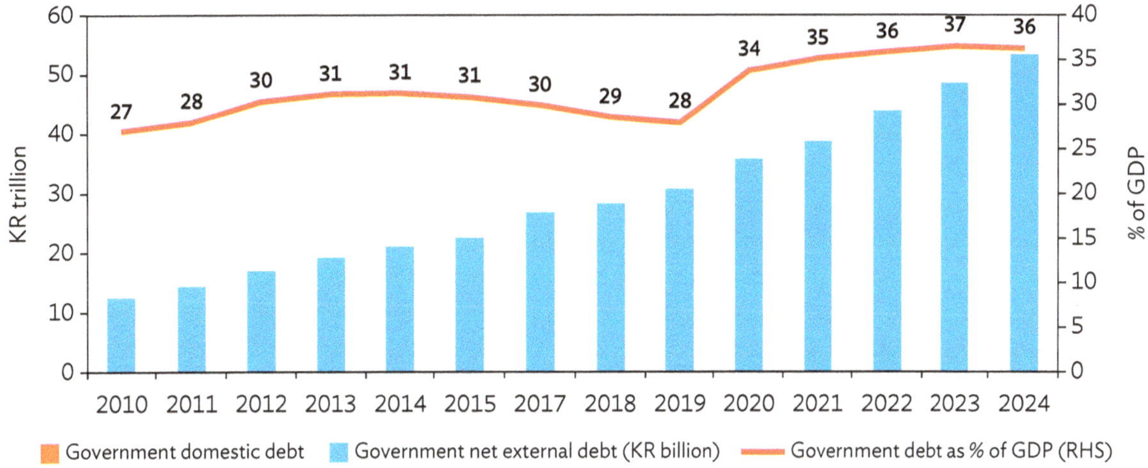

GDP = gross domestic product, RHS = right-hand scale.
Source: Asian Development Bank estimates.

The IMF's Article IV consultation for 2022 noted that while shocks to exports and growth may still affect the government's ability to manage its debt, the current risk of external or overall debt distress is low and will remain so if public debt is kept under control in the future, and if an increase in private debt does not lead to an increase in contingent liabilities. The country's debt service ratio remains low at about 2% of the value of exports of goods and services, and is thus considered sustainable. The IMF recommends that Cambodia maintain its fiscal stimulus measures to support economic recovery while ensuring debt sustainability and improving revenue mobilization and public financial management. In short, Cambodia's debt is sustainable and does not currently pose a concern or threaten macroeconomic stability.

External Sector Performance

Trade performance. Cambodia is one of the most open economies in Asia and the Pacific. The country's trade has grown steadily as its engagement in the global economy deepened. From 2010 to 2019, its exports of goods and services grew by an annual average of 16%, as imports grew by 15%.

However, Cambodia's trade is highly concentrated in terms of export composition, export markets, and import sources. While the composition of Cambodia's exports has changed significantly, they remain heavily concentrated in a few manufactures. Garments and footwear continued to make up almost 60% of Cambodia's exports in 2021, albeit down from a little over 80% in 2015. Other important exports in 2021 were machinery and electronic components, plastics and rubber, and agricultural products (Figure 8). Cambodia's main imports in 2021 were transportation equipment, textiles, and machinery and electronic components (Figure 9).

Figure 8: Cambodia's Export Products, 2015 and 2021
(% of exports)

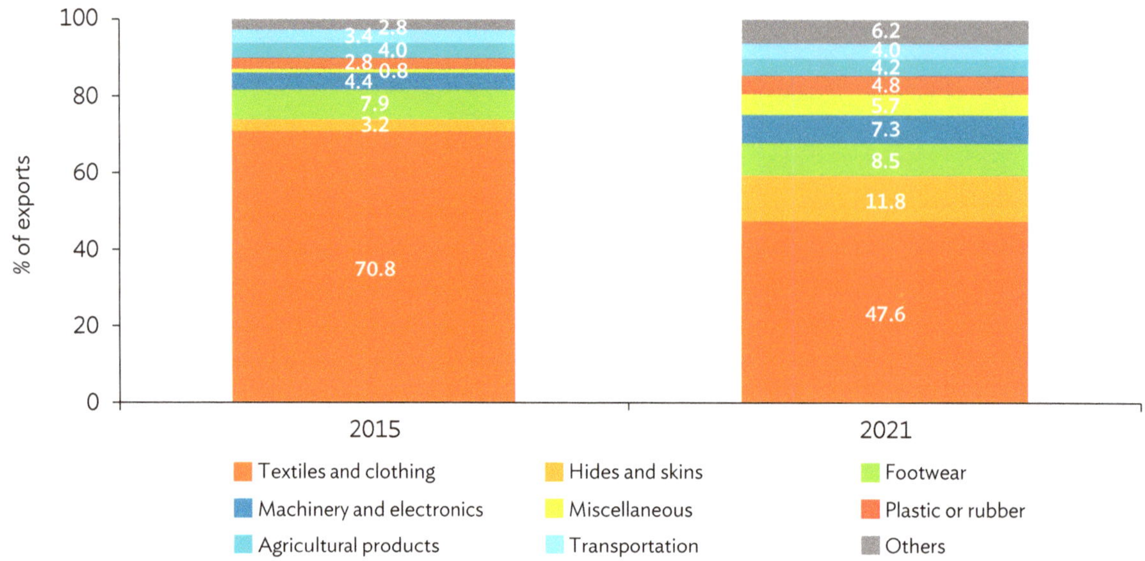

Source: World Bank. World Integrated Trade Solution. https://wits.worldbank.org/ (accessed 11 December 2023).

Figure 9: Cambodia's Import Products, 2015 and 2021
(% of imports)

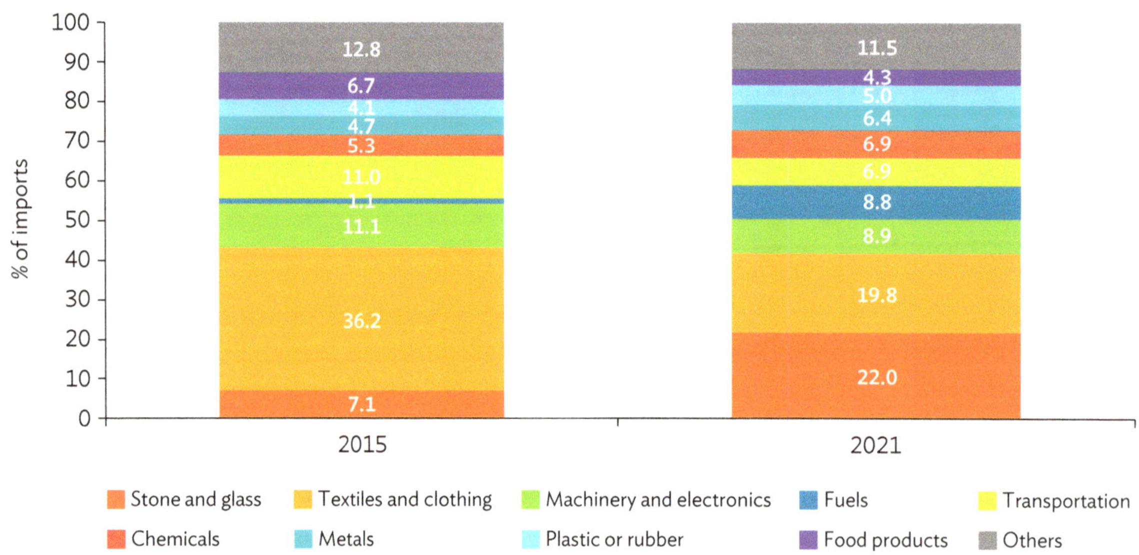

Source: World Bank. World Integrated Trade Solution. https://wits.worldbank.org/ (accessed 11 December 2023).

The US and the European Union together accounted for around 60% of the country's exports in 2021. Other major markets are Japan, the PRC, and Canada (Figure 10). The PRC is the country's top source of imports, followed by Thailand and Viet Nam, which together supply two-thirds of imports.

Figure 10: Cambodia's Export Markets, 2015 and 2021
(% of exports)

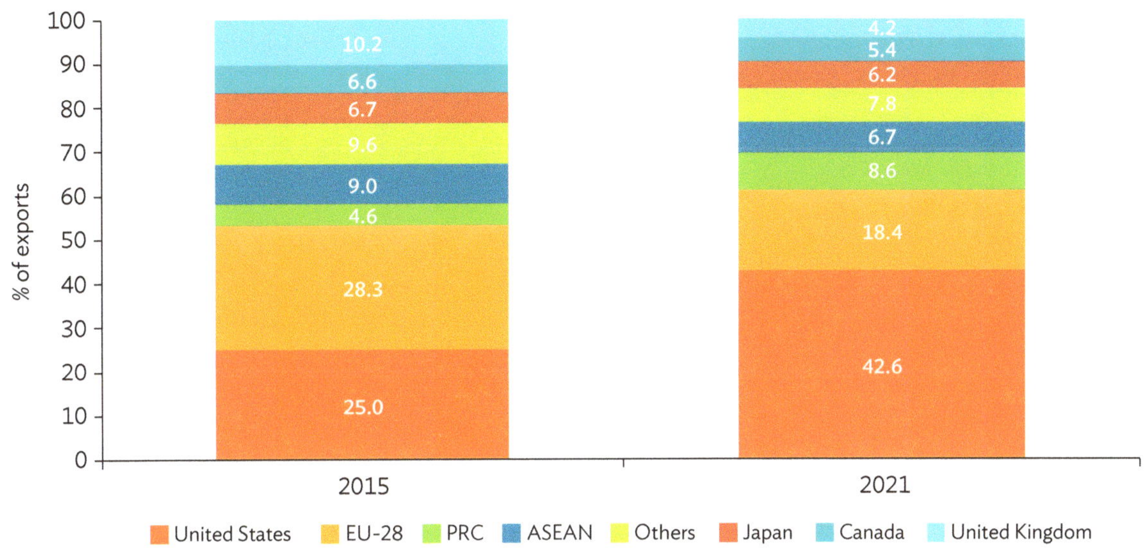

ASEAN = Association of Southeast Asian Nations, PRC = People's Republic of China, EU = European Union.
Source: World Bank. World Integrated Trade Solution. https://wits.worldbank.org/ (accessed 11 December 2023).

The low diversification of trade in terms of products or partners makes Cambodia vulnerable to external shocks, the implications of which are discussed in detail below when considering issues related to the sustainability and resilience of growth.

Trade policy. For the past 3 decades, Cambodia has been an open and outward-oriented economy with low barriers to international trade and other flows. This openness is the legacy of a policy framework established under the United Nations Transitional Authority in Cambodia, and Cambodian leaders have since made an explicit commitment to open trade and investment (Hill and Menon 2011, 2014). It was therefore not surprising when Cambodia became the first LDC to be admitted to the World Trade Organization in 2004.

Cambodia's accession to ASEAN in 1999 required it to participate in its first preferential or free trade agreement, the ASEAN Free Trade Area, which later became the ASEAN Trade in Goods Agreement. Membership in ASEAN also pulled Cambodia into various ASEAN+1 free trade agreements (FTAs) (Table 2). The ASEAN FTAs with the +3 countries of Japan, the PRC, and the Republic of Korea, and with Australia and New Zealand, were then brought together to form the Regional Comprehensive Economic Partnership, which came into effect on 1 January 2022. Like most other Asian countries, Cambodia has actively pursued bilateral FTAs. The most significant of these is the one with the PRC, which came into effect in 2022. Cambodia signed an FTA with the Republic of Korea in 2021 and began negotiations for one with Canada in the same year.

Table 2: Cambodia's 17 Free Trade Agreements and Their Status

Type	Proposed/Under Study	Negotiations Launched	Signed but Not Yet in Effect	Signed and in Effect
Bilateral			Cambodia–Korea Free Trade Agreement (2021)	Cambodia–People's Republic of China Free Trade Agreement (2022)
Plurilateral	• East Asia Free Trade Area (ASEAN+3) (2004) • Comprehensive Economic Partnership for East Asia (2005) • ASEAN-EU Free Trade Agreement (2007) • ASEAN–Pakistan Free Trade Agreement (2009) • ASEAN–Eurasian Economic Union Free Trade Agreement (2016) • Cambodia–Eurasian Economic Union FTA (2017)	ASEAN–Canada (2021)		• ASEAN Free Trade Area (1993) • ASEAN–People's Republic of China Comprehensive Economic Cooperation Agreement (2005) • ASEAN–Republic of Korea Comprehensive Economic Cooperation Agreement (2007) • ASEAN–Japan Comprehensive Economic Partnership (2008) • ASEAN–Australia and New Zealand Free Trade Agreement (2010) • ASEAN–India Comprehensive Economic Cooperation Agreement (2010) • ASEAN–Hong Kong, China Free Trade Agreement (2019) • Regional Comprehensive Economic Partnership (2022)

ASEAN = Association of Southeast Asian Nations, EU = European Union, FTA = free trade agreement.
Source: ADB. Asian Regional Integration Center FTA database. https://aric.adb.org/fta (accessed 25 April 2023).

Before the pandemic, Cambodia's current account deficit rose steadily from $2.7 billion in 2010 to $7.2 billion in 2019. As a share of GDP, the current account deficit averaged about 23% from 2010 to 2019. It narrowed to an estimated 9% in 2020 as imports shrank and exports of goods increased. In 2021, the current account deficit then soared to almost 46%, primarily because of faltering tourism and unexpectedly high imports of gold. As tourism begins to recover with the reopening, the current account deficit should narrow, although the pace of improvement could be influenced by the volatile gold trade (Figure 11).

Figure 11: Current Account Balance, 2010–2023
(% of GDP)

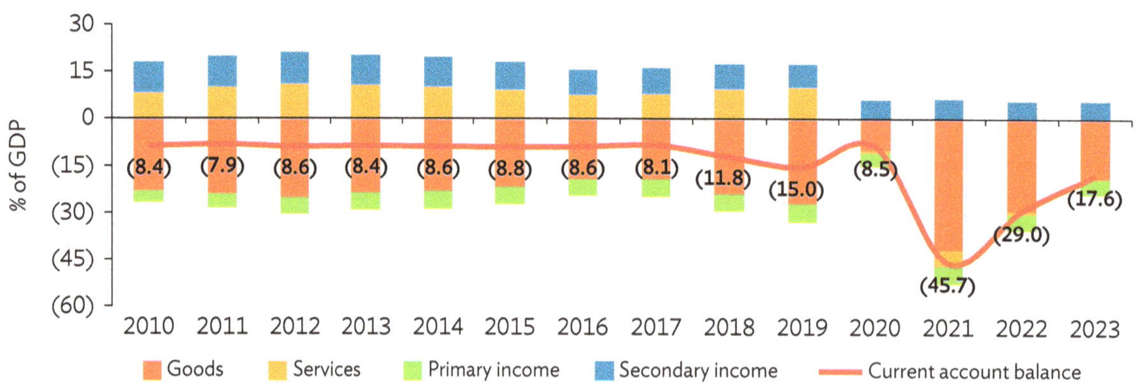

( ) = negative, GDP = gross domestic product.
Source: Asian Development Bank estimates.

Capital account. Cambodia's current account deficit was partly offset by capital and financial account surpluses, which were supported by strong inflows of foreign direct investment (FDI), remittances, and official development assistance. This has kept Cambodia's balance of payments relatively stable despite the challenges posed by COVID-19. Cambodia's capital and financial account averaged a modest surplus of about 2% of GDP from 2010 to 2019. In 2020, the capital account recorded a surplus of 1%.

The FDI inflow has contributed significantly to Cambodia's capital and financial account surplus. It reached a record high of nearly $3.7 billion in 2019, up from $1.4 billion in 2010. Most of this has been directed toward the finance sector, followed by the manufacturing and real estate sectors. The PRC is the largest source of FDI in Cambodia.

Cambodia's international reserves reached a record high of $21 billion at the end of 2020 and then fell slightly to $20 billion in 2021. Substantial foreign exchange reserves have prevented the exchange rate from coming under significant pressure. The IMF (2022) expected reserves to remain high and stable, covering for about 8 months of imports. Despite some challenges, Cambodia's overall external performance has remained strong.

Population, Labor, and Employment

Despite Cambodia's economic transformation in the past few decades, the vast majority of Cambodians still live in rural areas. The share of the rural population was still 75% in 2022, little changed from 80% in 2010 (Figure 12). Agriculture still employs the largest share of the workforce, although its share fell from 55% in 2010 to 39% in 2021. In the same period, the share of manufacturing rose from 16% to 25%, and the share of the service sector from 29% to 36% (Figure 13).

Figure 12: Rural and Urban Population, 2010–2022
(%)

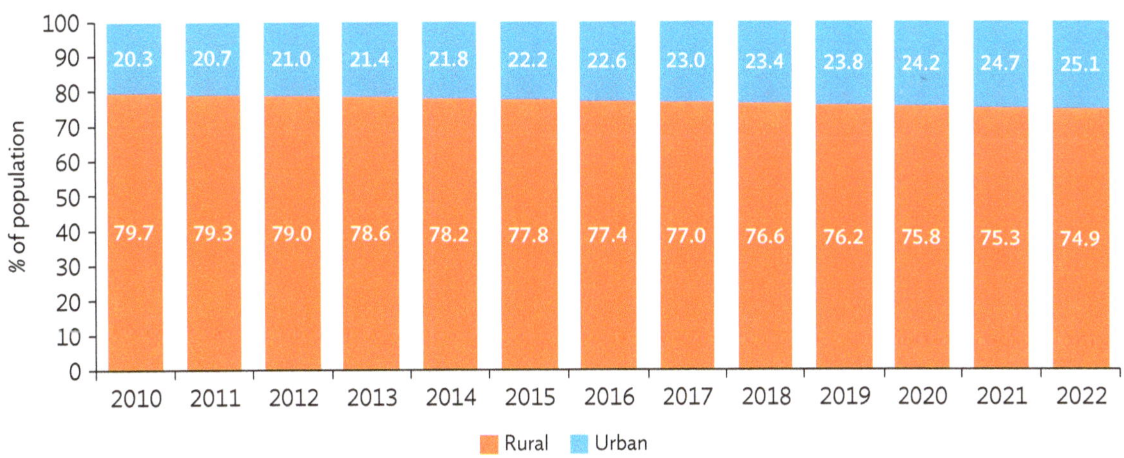

Source: World Bank. World Development Indicators. https://databank.worldbank.org/source/world-development-indicators# (accessed 11 December 2023).

Figure 13: Employment by Sector, 2010–2021
(%)

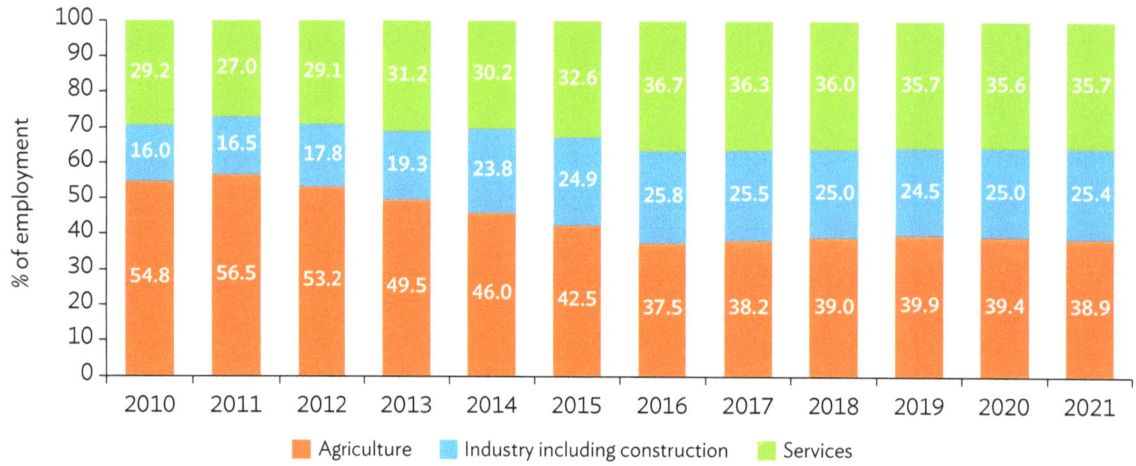

Source: World Bank. World Development Indicators. https://databank.worldbank.org/source/world-development-indicators# (accessed 11 December 2023).

Demographic trends are providing Cambodia with a large and expanding labor force estimated at 9.1 million workers in 2021, with a labor force participation rate of 83.7% (National Institute of Statistics, various years).

Decades of strong economic growth have created a lot of jobs in the country. The International Labour Organization (ILO) estimates unemployment at 4% in 2019. Unemployment has certainly increased during the pandemic and may not have been fully reversed yet. However, the main concern in the Cambodian labor market is not quantity, but quality. Informal employment and underemployment remain widespread, with most workers employed in low-productivity and low-wage sectors such as agriculture and informal services. According to the ILO, 89% of Cambodian workers were employed in the informal sector in 2019, working in low-paying jobs without social protection or job security. Worktime underemployment was reported at 11% in 2019.

Cambodia's labor productivity still lags behind many countries in the region. In 2020, labor productivity per worker was only \$2.89, well below \$14.78 in Thailand and \$12.04 in Indonesia, and less than half of \$6.58 in the peer economy of Viet Nam.[2]

One of the biggest challenges facing Cambodia is improving its human capital and skills base. (This critical constraint on inclusive growth is discussed in detail in the chapter on constraints on diversification.) The government recognizes this challenge and has set goals to improve jobs and upskill its population in the Pentagon Strategy (Phase I), the National Employment Policy, 2015–2025, and Cambodia's Industrial Development Policy, 2015–2025. Cambodia has taken steps to address some of the problems in the labor market. These include implementing labor regulations and programs to improve the quality of education and providing training to improve workers' skills and productivity. However, more needs to be done, and fundamental reform is required (Chapter 3).

2 ADB estimates in constant 2017 prices, purchasing power parity, using the Asian Productivity Organization database.

The pandemic has had a significant impact on employment in Cambodia. The ILO estimated the loss of working hours at 1.1 million full-time jobs in 2020, 1.3 million in 2021, and 1.0 million in 2022, mostly in the tourism, manufacturing, and construction sectors. The closure of hotels, restaurants, and other tourism-related businesses significantly undermined employment in services, particularly among low-skilled workers. The pandemic therefore forced migrant workers in urban areas or overseas to return to their home provinces, reversing a long-term trend of net out-migration from rural areas.

Poverty and Human Development

Despite its significant economic growth, Cambodia remains one of the poorest countries in Southeast Asia, with a gross national income per capita of $1,349 in 2021, measured in constant 2015 dollars. Although Cambodia is still classified as an LDC by the United Nations, it could meet the criteria in 2024 for graduation from LDC status as early as 2027.

The government has implemented programs and policies to boost economic growth and reduce poverty, especially in rural areas. These initiatives include the Cambodia Sustainable Development Goals; Second National Strategy for Food Security and Nutrition, 2019–2023; Agricultural Sector Strategic Development Plan, 2019–2023; and National Action Plan for Zero Hunger Challenge in Cambodia, 2016–2025. Further, the government's establishment of the Social Protection Policy Framework underscores its commitment to establishing a financially sustainable system that addresses poverty while promoting human capital development. These initiatives have included cash transfers, rural infrastructure development, and improvements in health care and education. The share of Cambodians living below the national poverty line of KR4,618, which is equal to $1.04 per day, declined from 33.8% in 2009 to 17.8% in 2019 (Figure 14). The government aimed to reduce poverty further to below 10% by 2023.

Figure 14: Poverty Rate, 2009, 2014, and 2019
(%)

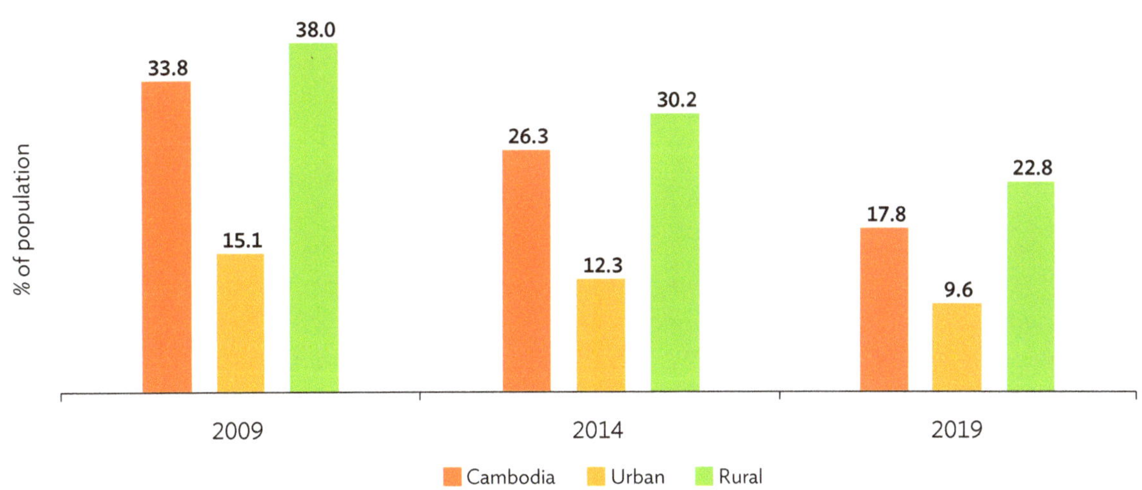

Source: World Bank. Cambodia Poverty Assessment 2022.

Despite notable progress in recent years, poverty is still pervasive, particularly in rural areas. In 2019, the poverty rate in rural areas was 22.8% using the national poverty line, which was more than double 9.6% in urban areas (Figure 14). A similar disparity can be seen in food poverty, which has declined across the country but remains much higher in rural areas (Figure 15). While there have been notable achievements in reducing food and extreme poverty through economic growth and various targeted government programs,[3] a significant proportion of the population remains vulnerable. The Asian Development Bank (ADB) estimates that about 30% of Cambodians are "near poor" or vulnerable to being pushed into poverty by illness, disasters, or economic shocks. Using the World Bank's higher poverty line of $3.20 a day, about a third of the population is below this (Karamba, Tong, and Salcher 2022).

Figure 15: Food Poverty, 2009, 2014, and 2019
(%)

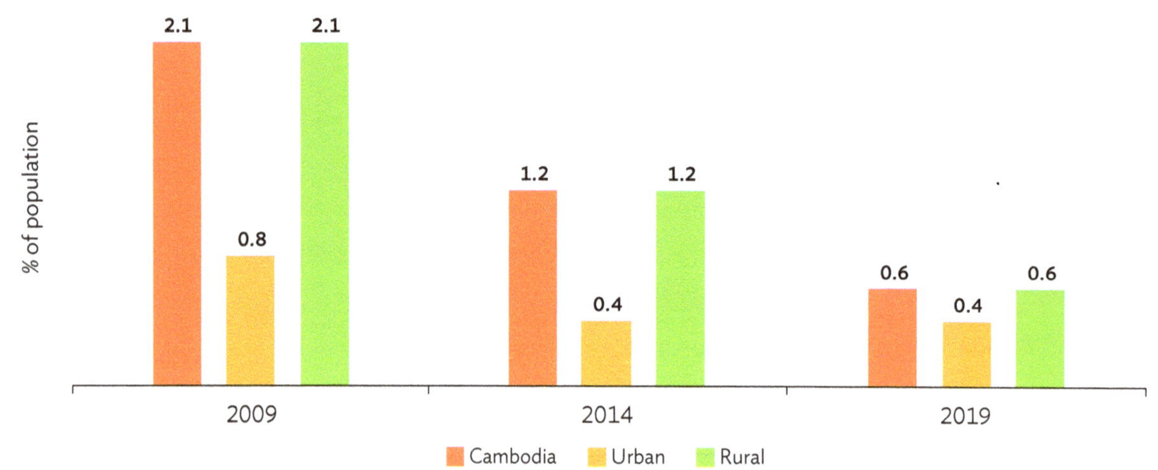

Source: World Bank. Cambodia Poverty Assessment 2022.

More worryingly, income inequality, as measured by the Gini coefficient, worsened from 29.9 in 2014 to 32.2 in 2019, after remaining fairly stable over the previous 5-year period (Figure 16). Further, the data on consumption per capita by quintile show that the average monthly consumption by the bottom fifth increased by only 23% in 2019/2020 compared with 2014, while that of the top fifth increased by 60%. This is a drastic reversal compared to the period from 2009 to 2014, when the average monthly consumption of the bottom 20% rose by 71% and that of the top fifth by 28% (Table 3). It is likely that inequality in asset and wealth is also high and rising, but data on these measures are sparse.

Progress in reducing poverty and improving human development outcomes was reversed under the pandemic, with an estimated 460,000 people falling into poverty in 2020 and raising the poverty rate by 2.8 percentage points. The World Bank estimated that without government intervention, the pandemic would have increased poverty by 4.7 percentage points in 2020, undoing 3 years of progress in poverty reduction.

3 These include, for instance, the Social Health Equity Fund, Food Reserve Program, Nutrition Program, and School Feeding Program.

Figure 16: Gini Coefficient 2009, 2014, and 2019

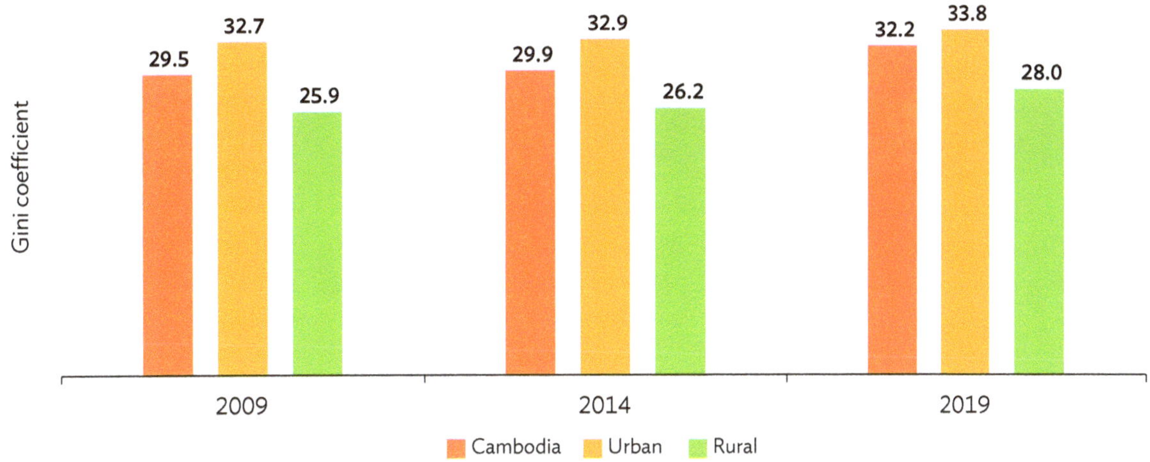

Source: World Bank. Cambodia Poverty Assessment 2022.

Table 3: Consumption per Capita by Quintile, 2009, 2014, and 2019

	KR '000			% of Total			% Increase	
Quintile	2009	2014	2019	2009	2014	2019	2014 vs. 2009	2019 vs. 2014
Lowest fifth	97	166	204	8	9	7.7	71	23
Second fifth	144	240	304	11	13	11.5	67	27
Middle fifth	192	309	403	15	17	15.3	61	30
Fourth fifth	269	407	559	21	22	21.2	51	37
Highest fifth	570	731	1,166	45	39	44.2	28	60

Note: Values are monthly averages.
Source: Ministry of Planning, National Institute of Statistics. Cambodia Socio-economic Surveys, 2009, 2014, and 2019/2020.

Cambodia's performance on the Human Development Index has likewise suffered a reversal in recent years. From 1990 to 2018, the index showed a positive trend, increasing from 0.378 to 0.598. However, from 2018 to 2021, it decreased slightly to 0.593, categorizing Cambodia as a country with medium human development, ranked 146th out of 191 countries in terms of human capital development. Significant gaps remain in the areas of health and education. Cambodia performed poorly in the Global Competitiveness Report 2019, ranking 119th out of 141 economies in terms of overall competitiveness.

3 Addressing Critical Constraints on Inclusive Growth

Context

Limited diversification. The Cambodian economy has been transformed in many ways since it started embracing market-oriented reforms more than 3 decades ago. However, structural change and diversification of the economy has been rather constrained during this period (Appendix). As mentioned, the share of services in GDP remained unchanged at about 35% from 1995 to 2021. While this partly reflected the impact of the pandemic on tourism, it also highlighted that the sectoral shifts had featured mainly shrinking agriculture and expanding manufacturing sectors. More recently, intra-sector changes have taken place within manufacturing and agriculture. Nevertheless, the persistent lack of economic diversification suggests that the key constraints on making growth more inclusive are still being felt.

In other words, these long-standing and binding constraints did little to limit Cambodia's ability to grow rapidly over the 2 decades before the pandemic. They did, however, constrain the quality and inclusiveness of economic growth. This is a compelling reason to address these constraints, which is key to realizing Cambodia's aspirations and long-term vision. Moreover, the previous drivers of rapid growth in Cambodia may not last into the future.

Rapid growth despite little diversification. For a number of reasons, Cambodia has been able to grow rapidly despite many constraints and a general lack of diversification. First, trade preferences, in particular the Generalized System of Preferences provided by the US and the Everything but Arms preferences provided by the European Union, have enabled strong growth in garment exports. Second, tourists drawn most significantly by Angkor Wat, have ensured that tourism contributes about 12% to GDP directly and much more indirectly. Tourism's biggest contribution is employment. It is estimated that the number of jobs created by tourism in one way or another exceeds 30% of all jobs in Cambodia (World Travel and Tourism Council 2018). Cambodia has also received large inflows of official development assistance, and its strategic location has allowed it to benefit from international political and economic dynamics. Cambodia's close ties with the PRC, both real and perceived, have garnered it greater attention and support from other regional partners.

As Cambodia continues to develop, some of these advantages will fall away as victims of Cambodia's success. Graduation from LDC status, expected in this decade, will extinguish unilateral trade preferences and lead to a further decline in flows of official development assistance. The saturation of tourist flows in Siem Reap and the question of sustainability of the tourism market in general are further concerns for the future. Cambodia will thus need to look for new drivers of growth, which means addressing the critical constraints on economic diversification and more inclusive growth.

The Objective: Inclusive Growth That Produces Decent and Sustainable Jobs and Returns

All long-term strategic plans and their underlying economic policies aim implicitly or explicitly to support inclusive economic growth. Such growth must generate decent and sustainable jobs in manufacturing and services. It must also provide fair and sustainable returns for the self-employed in agriculture or in micro, small, and medium-sized enterprises (MSMEs) in all sectors, whether formal or informal. This type of growth is bottom-up, empowering the working-age population through education and skills development and equal opportunities to participate in generating growth, regardless of class, gender, or location.

Decent jobs are those that provide a fair income that is at least equal to the minimum wage and is increased over time to keep pace with the cost of living and productivity improvement. Such jobs must protect workers' rights and provide a safe working environment. To make this possible and ensure equal opportunities and treatment for all, workers must be encouraged and helped to shift from informal to formal employment, and undocumented migrant labor must be regularized to make it legal. Sustainable jobs are those that provide safe and secure working conditions that facilitate extended working life in line with longer life expectancy. They are generally found in industries that are resilient to shocks, whether the shock is technological advance, climate change, or whatever. Sustainability requires workers who are able to respond to change by equipping them with the skills and flexibility needed to migrate from shrinking industries into expanding sectors of the economy.

The Means: Diversification

The government has highlighted the need to diversify the economy for more resilient growth in its various long-term strategic plans, including the previous Rectangular Strategy (Phase IV) and the current Pentagon Strategy (Phase I). Diversification is not an end in itself, but the means for achieving the ultimate objective of generating economic growth that delivers decent and sustainable jobs and returns. What is the link between diversification and inclusive growth?

Diversification and Inclusive Growth

Diversification entails structural change, and to achieve inclusive growth, structural change must deliver better and more sustainable jobs.

Diversification or structural change thus entails reallocating factors of production from one economic activity to another as warranted. This has long been a central aspect of development. It dates back at least to Kaldor (1967), who emphasized economic sectors interacting to generate growth in modern economies, arguing in particular that manufacturing is the main engine of growth. Kuznets (1971) identified structural transformation as one of six characteristics of modern economic growth. More recently, Herrendorf, Rogerson, and Valentinyi (2013) argued that diversification and the resulting change in the sector composition of GDP are critical for understanding income convergence, productivity growth, and wage outcomes—all of which are important determinants of inclusive growth.

Understanding inclusive growth requires consideration of how it is linked with several dimensions of diversification and changes in the composition of GDP. Moving horizontally into higher-value products or activities must be distinguished from moving vertically up the value chain to products or activities with more value added. While a horizontal shift to higher-value products usually entails diversification across sectors, a vertical shift takes place within a sector. The implications of intra-sector versus inter-sector diversification are critical for understanding development transitions and their ability to make growth more inclusive. They are considered in more detail below.

Intra-Sector Versus Inter-Sector Diversification

To understand how diversification can facilitate inclusive growth, it is useful to break down restructuring into two modes: intra-sector and inter-sector. A sector is defined here as one of the three broad economic pursuits: agriculture, manufacturing, and services.

In the early phase of industrialization in developing countries like Cambodia, the rural–urban migration of labor is a response to difference in factor rewards. The result is inter-sector diversification, where the GDP share of agriculture declines while the shares of manufacturing and services increase. As noted above, the share of agriculture in Cambodia has fallen by half over the past 25 years to less than a quarter of GDP, most of it replaced by a higher share for industry, mainly manufacturing and construction.

In this type of inter-sector diversification, workers move horizontally from low-value agriculture to higher-value manufacturing and construction. Low-skilled workers learn few if any new skills, but still achieve a one-off increase in productivity from an output with higher value. Low-skilled workers' incomes rise with minimal adjustment costs as they require little training to perform new, but still low-skilled, tasks in manufacturing and construction.

While inter-sector diversification changes the relative shares of the individual sectors in GDP, intra-sector diversification, by contrast, can leave the shares of the big three economic sectors little changed, with the shifts taking place mainly within each of them.

Cross-country comparisons suggest that Cambodia may have already realized most of the benefits from the moving of workers from agriculture to manufacturing or services. While the inter-sector transfer of factors of production across sectors increases productivity, this boost is likely to be one-off and unable to sustain growth over time. For example, while rice farmers may increase the value of their output per hour by moving to an electronics factory and assembling wire harnesses, it is unlikely that they will assemble the harnesses markedly more efficiently over time.

Future productivity growth requires a new phase of structural transformation featuring intra-sector specialization. This second phase involves the vertical reallocation of factors to produce higher value-added goods within existing supply chains. In Cambodia, this would require greater involvement of the private sector to generate new forms of involvement in global manufacturing supply chains. Unlike in the early phase of industrialization, this upgrading process is unlikely to happen spontaneously, but will require government intervention and policy reforms. It will also likely require new forms of investment, particularly FDI with embedded technologies, and skilled labor will be required to facilitate intra-sector specialization and upgrading. The opportunities for Cambodia to diversify its product mix and export basket through structural transformation can be identified in the short and long run using product space analysis (Appendix).

The Constraints: Human Capital, Business Costs, and Resilience and Sustainability

What constrains greater economic diversification that would achieve more inclusive growth? Two types of constraints on structural change need to be addressed. The first is when skills mismatches leave human capital deficient. The second is when the cost of doing business is too high to allow for private sector development or domestic and foreign investment.

To sustain growth, another set of constraints on resilience and sustainability must be addressed. Enhanced versatility is needed to respond to disruption, manage its consequences, and keep growth drivers from stalling and thus ensure sustainability. Sustainability and resilience depend on addressing the impacts of (i) climate change and other environmental pressures; (ii) financial, health, and other shocks or crises; and (iii) technological change, especially with acceleration toward a digital economy. Improving the sustainability of growth and its drivers requires diversified sources of FDI, export markets, and import sources, to avoid putting too many eggs in one basket.

Human Capital

Improving human capital and skills is a constant challenge for any economy, but especially for developing countries, and not least for Cambodia given its traumatic history. Although significant progress has been made in recent decades, the education system and skills development still face fundamental challenges. There is an urgent need to improve the quality of education at all levels, starting with primary and secondary schools. The 2022 Programme for International Student Assessment (PISA) results show that despite improvements since 2017, Cambodia lags behind its ASEAN peers in mathematics, science, and reading (Figure 17).Cambodia also lags behind in the share of its labor force with advanced education (Figure 18).

Figure 17: PISA Mathematics, Science, and Reading Scores at Age 15, Comparing Cambodia with Regional Peers, 2022

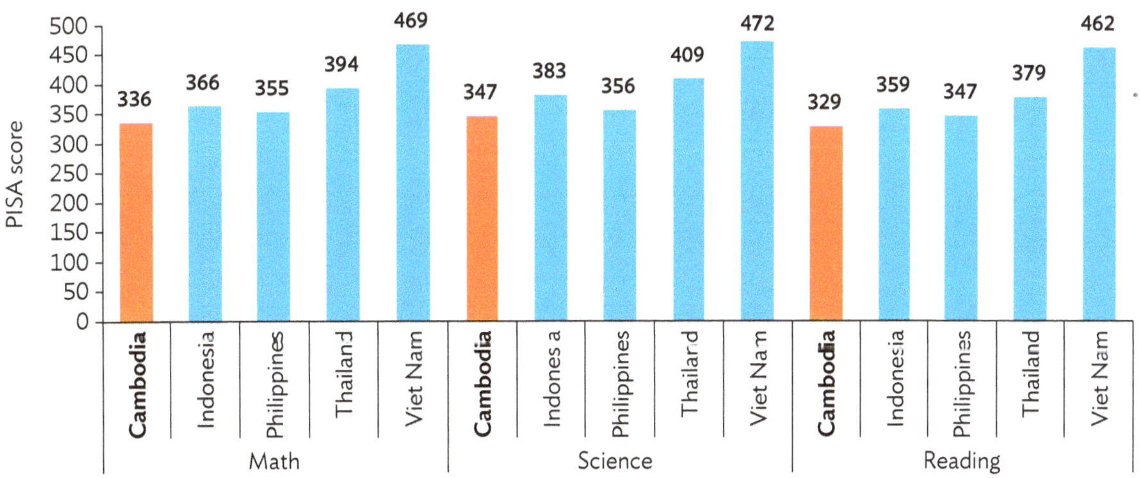

PISA = Programme for International Student Assessment.
Notes: Caution is required when comparing PISA 2022 estimates for Viet Nam with those for other economies as strong linkage with international PISA reading scores could not be established. Some apparent differences may not be statistically significant.
Sources: Organisation for Economic Co-operation and Development. Programme for International Student Assessment (PISA) 2022; PISA 2022 Results, Volume 1, Reader's Guide, and Annex 4.

Figure 18: Labor Force Educational Attainment, 2015 Versus 2021
(% of working-age population)

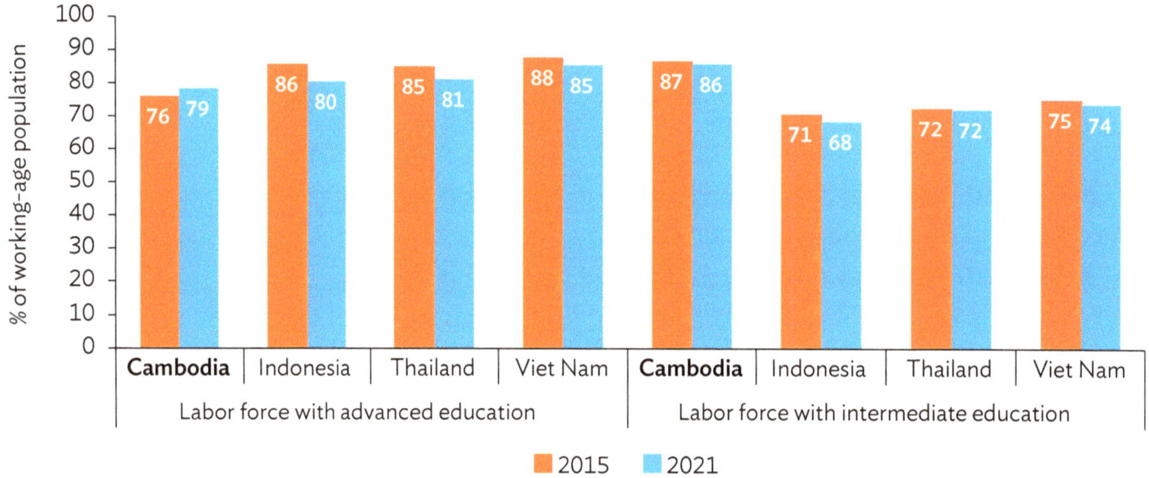

Source: World Bank. World Development Indicators. https://databank.worldbank.org/source/world-development-indicators# (accessed 11 December 2023).

These challenges predate the pandemic and will only have been exacerbated by prolonged closure of schools, with poor people disproportionately affected and falling even further behind (Menon 2020). There is already evidence that school closures have increased "learning poverty" quite significantly, especially among children from poor households.[4] Cambodia needs to reverse the decline during the pandemic and address long-standing challenges to increase retention rates in secondary education and improve post-secondary vocational education training.

Business Costs

Cambodia has always scored poorly in the World Bank's composite Ease of Doing Business Index (Table 4). Before the index was discontinued in 2020, Cambodia usually ranked in Southeast Asia above only the Lao People's Democratic Republic (Lao PDR) and Myanmar. The high cost of doing business in Cambodia stems from a number of shortcomings, most notably poor physical infrastructure and logistics (Table 5). Despite considerable investment in roads and other transport infrastructure from the government, multilateral institutions, and bilateral partners, notably the PRC through its Belt and Road Initiative, transport network expansion has not kept pace with economic growth, even during the pandemic-induced slowdown. This impinges on the country's economic competitiveness. Red tape, inadequate port facilities, and other inefficiencies also undermine trade. Cambodia compares poorly with its neighbors in terms of the time and cost required to export and import (Table 6).

4 Learning poverty means being unable to read and understand a simple text at the age of 10. This indicator is calculated based on the share of children who, according to schools, have not achieved minimum reading proficiency and is adjusted by the percentage of children who are out of school and are therefore assumed not to read proficiently. The World Bank (2021) found in a major study that the share of children in low- and middle-income countries suffering from learning poverty has risen from 53% before the pandemic to possibly as high as 70% after prolonged school closures and the failure of remote learning to provide full learning continuity.

Table 4: Ease of Doing Business: Cambodia Versus Comparator Countries, 2015–2019

Indicator	Country	2015	2016	2017	2018	2019
Ease of doing business rank (1 = most business-friendly regulations)	Cambodia	...	...	...	...	144
	Lao PDR	...	...	...	...	154
	Thailand	...	...	...	...	21
	Viet Nam	...	...	...	...	70
	Lower-middle income	...	...	...	...	...
Ease of doing business score (0–100, worst to best)	Cambodia	52.9	53.2	53.4	53.8	53.8
	Lao PDR	48.2	49.1	50.0	49.8	50.8
	Thailand	71.9	72.8	78.5	79.5	80.1
	Viet Nam	62.6	65.3	67.0	68.6	69.8
	Lower-middle income	52.8	53.7	54.8	56.1	57.4
New business density (new registrations per 1,000 people aged 15–64)	Cambodia	0.4	0.4	0.5	0.7	0.9
	Lao PDR	0.1	0.1	0.1	0.1	0.2
	Thailand	0.9	1.0	1.1	1.5	1.5
	Viet Nam	1.1	1.3	1.5	1.6	1.7
	Lower-middle income	0.3	0.3	0.4	0.4	0.4

... = data not available, Lao PDR = Lao People's Democratic Republic.
Source: World Bank. Ease of Doing Business. https://databank.worldbank.org/source/world-development-indicators# (accessed 25 April 2023).

Table 5: Logistics Performance Index: Cambodia Versus Comparators, Selected Years

Index Feature	Country	2010	2012	2014	2016	2018	2022
Overall	Cambodia	2.4	2.6	2.7	2.8	2.6	2.4
	Lao PDR	2.5	2.5	2.4	2.1	2.7	2.4
	Thailand	3.3	3.2	3.4	3.3	3.4	3.5
	Viet Nam	3.0	3.0	3.2	3.0	3.3	3.3
	Lower-middle income	2.6	2.5	2.6	2.5	2.6	2.6
Ability to track and trace consignments	Cambodia	2.5	2.8	2.9	2.7	2.5	2.8
	Lao PDR	2.5	2.5	2.2	1.8	2.9	2.4
	Thailand	3.4	3.2	3.5	3.2	3.5	3.6
	Viet Nam	3.1	3.2	3.2	2.8	3.5	3.4
	Lower-middle income	2.6	2.5	2.6	2.5	2.6	2.6
Competence and quality of logistics services	Cambodia	2.3	2.5	2.7	2.6	2.4	2.4
	Lao PDR	2.1	2.5	2.3	2.1	2.7	2.4
	Thailand	3.2	3.0	3.3	3.1	3.4	3.5
	Viet Nam	2.9	2.7	3.1	2.9	3.4	3.2
	Lower-middle income	2.4	2.5	2.5	2.5	2.5	2.6
Ease of arranging competitively priced shipments	Cambodia	2.2	2.6	2.8	3.1	2.8	2.3
	Lao PDR	2.7	2.4	2.5	2.2	2.7	2.3
	Thailand	3.3	3.2	3.3	3.4	3.5	3.5
	Viet Nam	3.0	3.1	3.2	3.1	3.2	3.3
	Lower-middle income	2.7	2.5	2.6	2.5	2.5	2.6

continued on next page

Table 5 *continued*

Index Feature	Country	2010	2012	2014	2016	2018	2022
Efficiency of customs clearance process	Cambodia	2.3	2.3	2.7	2.6	2.4	2.2
	Lao PDR	2.2	2.4	2.4	1.8	2.6	2.3
	Thailand	3.0	3.0	3.2	3.1	3.1	3.3
	Viet Nam	2.7	2.7	2.8	2.8	3.0	3.1
	Lower-middle income	2.2	2.3	2.4	2.3	2.4	2.4
Frequency with which shipments reach consignee within scheduled or expected time	Cambodia	2.8	3.0	2.8	3.3	3.2	2.7
	Lao PDR	3.2	2.8	2.7	2.7	2.8	2.8
	Thailand	3.7	3.6	4.0	3.6	3.8	3.5
	Viet Nam	3.4	3.6	3.5	3.5	3.7	3.3
	Lower-middle income	3.2	3.0	2.9	2.9	2.9	2.9
Quality of trade and transport-related infrastructure	Cambodia	2.1	2.2	2.6	2.4	2.1	2.1
	Lao PDR	2.0	2.4	2.2	1.8	2.4	2.3
	Thailand	3.2	3.1	3.4	3.1	3.1	3.7
	Viet Nam	2.6	2.7	3.1	2.7	3.0	3.2
	Lower-middle income	2.2	2.3	2.3	2.4	2.3	2.4

Lao PDR = Lao People's Democratic Republic.
Note: Ranking is 1–5, low–high.
Source: World Bank. World Development Indicators. https://databank.worldbank.org/source/world-development-indicators# (accessed 11 December 2023).

Table 6: Cost and Time to Export and Import—Cambodia Versus Comparator Countries, 2019

Indicator	Cambodia	Lao PDR	Thailand	Viet Nam	Lower-Middle Income
Cost to export, border compliance ($)	375	140	223	290	439
Cost to export, documentary compliance ($)	100	235	96.9	139.2	142
Cost to import, border compliance ($)	240	224	233	373	542
Cost to import, documentary compliance ($)	120	115	44	183	211
Time to export, border compliance (hours)	48	9	44	55	70
Time to export, documentary compliance (hours)	132	60	11	50	61
Time to import, border compliance (hours)	8	11	50	56	110
Time to import, documentary compliance (hours)	132	60	4	76	72

Lao PDR = Lao People's Democratic Republic.
Notes: Border compliance captures the time and cost associated with compliance with the economy's customs regulations and with regulations relating to other inspections that are mandatory in order for the shipment to cross the economy's border, as well as the time and cost for handling that takes place at its port or border. Documentary compliance captures the time and cost associated with compliance with the documentary requirements of all government agencies of the origin economy, the destination economy, and any transit economies.
Source: World Bank. Ease of Doing Business. https://databank.worldbank.org/source/world-development-indicators# (accessed 25 April 2023).

Energy costs are another major constraint inhibiting growth and development. The high cost of electricity compared with neighboring economies and its unreliable supply add to the cost of doing business and can deter domestic and foreign investment. While this affects consumers and all kinds of producers, it hits manufacturing the hardest (Warr and Menon 2016).

Poor access to finance and high costs remain problematic in Cambodia despite notable progress in extending financial services to the population through better access to credit and the proliferation of mobile banking services. Microfinance institutions (MFIs) have driven financial inclusion in Cambodia, providing a range of financial services to low-income and rural populations. However, access to formal financial services is still only moderate, with about one-third of adults still without them. Despite a proliferation of bank and nonbank financial institutions, financing costs remain high, especially for MFIs. Almost all lending is secured by land or similar collateral.

Constraints on governance and institutional capacity also impinge on the cost of doing business. If these factors are left unaddressed, they will continue to undermine corporate competitiveness, the quality of public service delivery, and access to assets and opportunities.[5] As they also worsen risk and uncertainty, low business confidence can deter investment.

Resilience and Sustainability

As an LDC and a small, open economy in transition, Cambodia is particularly vulnerable to domestic and international shocks. A pressing need for Cambodia is to acquire versatility in managing and responding to disruptions to strengthen its resilience. The risk of contagion from international economic or financial crises is increasing as Cambodia becomes more integrated into the regional and global economy through trade and investment. As mentioned earlier, this was evident during the GFC when growth in Cambodia slowed down to almost zero, dragged down by its heavy reliance on the US export market. The pandemic is a more recent reminder of how exogenous events such as a global public health crisis can almost paralyze an economy for years and reverse hard-won social gains. These events highlight the importance of engendering flexibility to deal with future shocks and thus build resilience.

Future disruption is most likely to come from three directions: (i) climate change and other environmental pressures; (ii) financial, health, and related shocks; and (iii) technological change, particularly with the acceleration toward a digital economy. As a recent joint report notes, the "polycrisis"—from climate change, the COVID-19 pandemic, and Russia's war in Ukraine—has severely disrupted energy, food, and finance systems in the region (UN, ADB, and UNDP 2023).[6] It has introduced new shocks and stresses and intensified familiar ones, especially for the most vulnerable groups in developing countries such as Cambodia.

5 Since the 1990s, the government has pursued three interrelated reform programs—for public financial management, decentralization, and public administration—to improve public sector management. The results have been mixed with only gradual improvement, especially in public financial management systems.

6 These pressures may appear to have emerged only recently, but they have been around for a considerable period of time. The Rectangular Strategy (Phase 2), for example, noted similar concerns brewing at its launch in 2008. It blamed climate change, global economic imbalance, and a continuing and deepening financial crisis for a global economic slowdown and higher oil price and food prices, and for consequent severe inflation in Cambodia in the short and medium term. These recurring challenges may best be viewed as long-standing in nature.

(i) *Climate Change and Other Environmental Pressures*

Southeast Asia is a region hard hit by climate change, where destructive storms, floods, heat waves, droughts, and other extreme and unpredictable weather events are expected to become more frequent. This will undermine the sustainability of future growth through its impact on agriculture and food production and other supply chains. Cambodia will be no exception. ADB (2023b) noted that Cambodia is highly vulnerable to climate change due to its geographic location, governance, and high dependence on climate-sensitive activities, and terrestrial ecosystems and natural capital.

Forest cover has shrunk dramatically because of uncontrolled land-use conversion, illegal logging, large-scale infrastructure development, and urbanization. Much of the remaining forest cover has been degraded by selective logging and unsustainable fuelwood extraction, as the overwhelming majority of the population still relies on traditional biomass for cooking, and even industry still uses fuelwood extensively.

Deforestation and agricultural expansion are worsening erosion and other forms of land degradation, reducing agricultural and fisheries productivity, weakening resilience to flooding. As fisheries are critical to food security, overfishing poses a further threat to rural communities, particularly in the Tonle Sap area.

Although Cambodia is still a low emitter of greenhouse gases, its emissions are rising because of deforestation, the expansion of rice cultivation, and the increasing energy needs of industry.

(ii) *Financial, Health, and Other Shocks or Crises*

Financial risks. As noted in Chapter 2, an open and facilitating approach to regulation has supported the rapid growth of the finance sector and lending in Cambodia. Given the scale of the economic impact of COVID-19, the NBC moved quickly to introduce a package of regulatory forbearance measures that restructured loans and deferred a planned increase in the capital conservation buffer. The restructuring program initially targeted sectors directly hit by COVID-19, but quickly expanded to include all private lending. Under the program, banks and MFIs were able to suspend loan interest and principal repayments and adjust repayment schedules without reclassifying loans as nonperforming. This enabled them to accommodate borrowers' need for flexibility without large-scale provisioning that would have constrained new lending.

A related concern is that some large locally owned banks are highly exposed to construction and real estate. The growth of the property sector has been accompanied by an increase in shadow banking by real-estate developers. If these worsening risks are not addressed urgently, a financial meltdown cannot be ruled out.

Health crisis. Health care resources in Cambodia lag those in its Southeast Asian neighbors, with lower life expectancy and higher rates of child malnutrition and infant and child mortality. Even before the pandemic, Cambodia had fallen behind on many of its Sustainable Development Goals (SDGs), making the country vulnerable and at risk and exacerbating the negative social impacts of the pandemic. Cambodia's health care resources are also lagging behind, according to the universal health coverage indicator of SDG 3 on health and well-being. The indicator measures average coverage—

of both the general population and the most disadvantaged—by essential services that prevent and treat disease. A score of just below 65 out of 100 in 2020 was insufficient to keep Cambodia on track to meet the target by 2030, and the pandemic has made it even less likely (Sustainable Development Report 2024).

When the pandemic broke out, Cambodia had already been falling short on its SDGs, which made the impact of the pandemic much worse than they otherwise would have been and held Cambodia back even further from achieving its SDGs. The potential for such vicious cycles must be removed to prepare Cambodia for the next health crisis. If that crisis comes too soon, Cambodia will be in a much worse position than it was at the time of COVID-19, precisely because of the devastating impact of the pandemic.

(iii) *Technological Change, Especially Acceleration Toward a Digital Economy*

One supposed silver lining attributed to the pandemic is the acceleration of the digital economy. Lockdowns and social distancing hastened the development and adoption of technologies in the Fourth Industrial Revolution that enabled working from home and remote learning. The pandemic highlighted how digital infrastructure enabled adaptation to lockdowns and minimized disruption to the economy and livelihoods.

While this acceleration is generally welcome, there will be short- and medium-term adjustment costs from labor churning from firm to firm and other labor market disruptions. Many low-skilled, repetitive jobs are being automated, starting in high-wage countries but quickly spreading to developing countries like Cambodia. While the net impact on jobs and the labor market over the long run is unclear, disruptive technologies are certain to lead to significant labor churning and job displacement in the short run.[7] Manyika et al. (2017) predicted that 800 million workers could be displaced, with about half of them needing new skills for new jobs. Low-skilled, repetitive jobs such as assembly line work are most at risk, and service jobs such as business process outsourcing will be increasingly threatened.

In addition to the greater risk of unemployment for low-skilled workers, the low wage growth for them compared to higher-skilled workers will deepen wage and income inequality (Nuesch 2007). The inadequate digital infrastructure in poor countries is exacerbated by unequal access within countries. Poor people in developing countries have less chance of gaining access to this infrastructure and, as a result, become even more marginalized. The inability of poor people to participate equally in remote learning threatens to perpetuate the intergenerational cycle of poverty and inequality.

Apart from worsening inequality within countries, the digital divide can widen development gaps between countries, further exacerbating the divide. Adoption rates for these technologies favor more developed economies, as countries' preparedness correlates negatively with their stage of development. Cambodia therefore faces a significant challenge to catch up with more developed countries and thus narrow the digital divide—the task made all the more difficult by its being a moving target.

7 For a discussion of how long-term impacts are likely to be net positive, see OECD (2016) and Menon (2019).

(iv) *Diversifying Trade and Investment Flows*

Cambodia's exports remain heavily concentrated, with garments and footwear making up some 70% of exports in 2022. A key objective of the government is to move away from heavy reliance on garment exports and participate in global supply chains for light manufacturing and the assembly of electronic and automotive parts and components. This is an example of diversification taking place entirely within manufacturing, involving intra-sector specialization within the inter-sector transfer.

Apart from commodity diversification, reducing vulnerability to shocks from certain countries requires diversification of export markets and import sources. As described in Chapter 2, Cambodia's trade partnerships lack diversity, with the US alone taking 43% of exports by value in 2021. When the GFC hit in 2008, Cambodia suffered one of the largest growth contractions in ASEAN because of its heavy reliance on the US market for its exports. The PRC now supplies almost a third of imports. While the case for diversifying export markets has long been made, the Russian invasion of Ukraine has highlighted the importance of pursuing the same type of diversification in imports. The current high concentration of both exports and imports makes Cambodia highly vulnerable to country-specific shocks.

(v) *Diversifying Sources of Foreign Direct Investment*

In addition to trade, diversifying sources of foreign investment is a good strategy to reduce risk and vulnerability to country-specific shocks. Excessive reliance on a single country for anything carries obvious risks. The PRC is now Cambodia's largest bilateral donor, creditor, and investor. As the PRC's growth begins to slow, diversifying economic partners can spread the risk.[8]

The diversification of sources of FDI can lead to a diversification of exports and vice versa. So far, the diversification of manufacturing away from the garment industry has been driven mainly by investments from Japan; the Republic of Korea; and Taipei,China. These investments are in global supply chains for electronics and automotive parts and components, which have so far focused on assembly and other light manufacturing in special economic zones in Phnom Penh and Poipet.

The PRC's investments have supported the expansion and upgrading of the garment and textile industries as well as agriculture and the development of much-needed physical infrastructure. However, they have not yet led to a diversification of manufacturing supply chains, even though the PRC is a major player in global supply chains.

8 Several commentators have argued that the government aims to diversify its sources of overseas development assistance. This is apparently being pursued to protect national sovereignty (Ngin 2022; Chheang 2021).

Driving Diversification

Broad Policy Approaches: Industrial Policy Versus Underlying Policy Reform

Two broad approaches achieve economic diversification, each closely associated with one of the two dimensions of industry or sector specialization described above. The first approach, which has recently become popular in some developed countries such as the US, is an industrial policy of "picking winners." In this approach, industries are cultivated by providing financial support and other forms of preferential treatment. The second approach directly addresses the underlying constraints that limit diversification. This approach pursues policy reforms that directly strengthen competitiveness to ensure a more efficient allocation of resources.

The two approaches need not be mutually exclusive.

A gradual, cautious approach is called for when a country like Cambodia diversifies through industrial policy. First, the degree of government intervention required to promote selective specialization can be daunting. Extensive support is needed in the form of government subsidies and other direct support, which may outstrip government revenue. A large-scale program of selective industrialization may therefore be infeasible or, if pursued nonetheless, may prove to be fiscally irresponsible and a burden on the economy.

If Cambodia chooses to pursue any kind of industrial policy, it should take a less interventionist approach that cultivates an enabling environment and addresses inefficiencies and market failures. Cambodia operates a generous program of fiscal and related incentives for qualified investment projects (QIPs) administered by the Council for the Development of Cambodia.[9] Tax holidays and other exemptions are designed to compensate for some of the additional costs of doing business in a transitional economy, and thus keep it competitive in attracting FDI.

Cambodia lacks the capacity to implement an industrial policy that goes beyond the current program of targeted incentives, despite recent increases in resource mobilization. The foregone-revenue costs of fiscal incentives and exemptions are significant to a country like Cambodia, yet these measures are necessary to maintain international competitiveness and reduce differences with the large informal sector, and thus encourage and gradually increase formalization.

Further steps to bring about structural change through massive subsidies would be fiscally irresponsible and unlikely to succeed. For the time being, Cambodia should retain its QIP incentives, but otherwise concentrate on policy reform that directly addresses underlying constraints blocking greater economic diversification.

9 For a discussion of the types of incentives available, qualifying criteria, and potential impacts, see Warr and Menon (2016).

Policy Reform to Address Underlying Constraints

The remainder of this chapter considers policy changes that directly address key constraints on more inclusive growth, particularly barriers to structural diversification. Such policies address deficiencies in human capital and skills, the high cost of doing business, and ways to improve economic resilience and sustainable growth in the face of disruption.

Human Capital

As noted above, there is an urgent need to improve the quality of education at all levels, not only in tertiary education and technical and vocational education and training (TVET). Governments and development partners tend to focus on tertiary education and TVET, overlooking the challenges in primary and secondary education. However, tertiary education and TVET can only be successful if students have a strong educational foundation. Otherwise, tertiary education and TVET are engaged in remedial efforts to make up for the shortcomings of secondary education rather than building on it. Quality improvement must be accompanied by easier access and higher retention rates.

A survey of firms operating in Cambodian special economic zones found that the average literacy of workers is very low (Warr and Menon 2016). The Japanese manufacturing firm Denso reported that more than 30% of new employees had never attended school, could neither read nor write, and had scant numeracy skills. Denso and other firms were willing to train them, but the low literacy and cognitive skills frustrated these efforts, leaving many workers with only the most routine manual tasks.

These fundamental challenges related to the quality of schooling and access and retention rates must be addressed concurrently with the challenges of skills development to reverse the pandemic's impact on employability. To avoid skills mismatches, Cambodia needs to invest in skills development and training in close collaboration with the private sector. TVET and tertiary education institutions need to coordinate with the private sector to better align their curricula more closely with employers' needs. Cambodia has an opportunity to leverage its young population and improve its competitiveness through innovation and technology by creating a better link between industry and education and promoting entrepreneurship. Finally, there is an urgent need to expand formal employment by addressing the various barriers that stand in its way, which in turn will allow social security systems to be strengthened.

Once these improvements are set in motion, the benefits could accrue as the improvements that gave the first generation of students a head start are reinforced when some of them become teachers and trainers for the next generation. A virtuous cycle can create its own momentum and bring intergenerational augmentation of skills and human capital at an increasingly rapid pace. The sooner this change in basic education is made, the earlier this virtuous cycle can get started and prepare Cambodia for future shocks and demands.

Business Costs

Transport and other infrastructure. While efforts to build much-needed transportation and other infrastructure have scored notable achievements over the past 2 decades, infrastructure demand in a rapidly transforming economy like Cambodia is a moving target. Despite recent improvements, the infrastructure deficit continues to add significantly to the cost of doing business. Investment needs to be properly ordered in the transport sector as in the whole economy. Within the transport sector, choke points such as low port capacity and costly logistics infrastructure should be overhauled as a priority. Intermodal connectivity should be a focus. As infrastructure development relies on foreign involvement—increasingly from the PRC under the Belt and Road Initiative—better vetting of project proposals needs to apply comprehensive cost-benefit analysis conducted by independent bodies.

Proposals for FDI are currently reviewed by the Council for the Development of Cambodia as part of the process to obtain QIP status and associated concessions, as noted above. While some of the criteria used to determine QIP status assess potential benefits to the local economy, the process is incomplete because it lacks a comprehensive cost-benefit framework or a system for prioritizing needs within specific sectors, notably transport infrastructure. A Cambodian foreign investment review board could operate as a non-statutory body with representatives from multiple ministries and other stakeholders, such as community leaders, academics, and the private sector, to assess individual proposals for the government in a purely advisory capacity. Interministerial representation would ensure that sector priorities are considered in the approval process. It should be supported by technically competent staff capable of undertaking comprehensive cost-benefit analysis as an input to the assessment.

Expensive electricity. The high cost of electricity in Cambodia is a key constraint on intra-sector diversification through vertical upgrading of supply chains in the electronics and automotive industries. It frustrates the transition from labor-intensive assembly to higher value addition through energy-intensive production of parts and components. Electricity is expensive in Cambodia mainly because of the way it is generated, as it is still heavily dependent on diesel and heavy fuel oil. Fragmented transmission and distribution systems add to the already high cost of electricity.

Some improvements have been made, however, and can be built upon. Reliance on diesel generators has gradually decreased. While higher oil prices were a major concern following the Russian invasion of Ukraine, the reduced reliance on oil imports and diesel fuel production has offset some of the higher petroleum costs. Grid expansion has had a positive impact, but a lot more investment is required. Increased investment is also needed in alternative energies, especially solar energy. There is significant potential to scale up investment in renewable energy and energy efficiency, taking advantage of Cambodia's abundant solar energy resources. This could significantly reduce business costs, especially for rural micro, small, and medium-sized enterprises (MSMEs) that are not connected to the electricity grid. The opportunities and challenges arising from the use of alternative energy are discussed in more detail below in the context of climate change.

Expensive finance. High financing costs, especially for smallholder farmers and other MSMEs, inhibit social advancement and poverty reduction. Poor access to formal finance reflects its high cost. The National Financial Inclusion Strategy, 2019–2025 aims to improve access to high-quality formal financial services; cut the percentage of women excluded from financial services from 27% to 13%; and increase the use of formal financial services in the general population from 59% to 70%. Formal financial inclusion is on track to meet the 2025 target (UNCDF 2021).

In recent years, the NBC has promoted digital payment systems to improve financial inclusion and make financial transactions more efficient. The Bakong payment system, a blockchain platform for digital payments, was launched in October 2020. The potential for digital innovation through fintech and blockchain offers significant opportunities for Cambodia's finance sector to improve inclusion and support economic growth. However, digital literacy and access to digital infrastructure are still low in rural areas, and will need to be improved to boost access to finance for poor people at a reasonable cost.

Other long-term development challenges need to be addressed to engender trust in the finance system, improve access, and lower its costs: governance and corruption, institutional strengthening, including the legal system, and developing the finance sector and capital markets.

Resilience and Sustainability

Cambodia needs to invest in measures that strengthen resilience by enabling versatility in response to disruptions emanating from (i) climate change and other environmental pressures; (ii) financial, health, and related shocks; and (iii) technological change, especially the acceleration toward a digital economy. Without timely mitigation and adaptation measures, the economic and social achievements of the past will be put at risk, as will the sustainability of future growth, affecting Cambodia's aspirations for the future.

(i) *Climate Change and Other Environmental Pressures*

The 2022 Notre Dame global adaptation index ranked Cambodia 149th out of 182 countries in its ability to strengthen its climate resilience. Climate change is already here, and its effects will worsen rapidly, urgently requiring countermeasures. Climate change threatens the livelihoods of millions of people and could derail long-term aspirations such as graduating to high-income country status by 2050. By that year, extreme weather events and rising temperatures, and labor productivity lost as a result, could shave as much as 10% off Cambodia's GDP (ADB 2023b). More frequent and severe floods and droughts are expected to have a massive impact on agriculture, and rising sea levels and saline intrusion will significantly impair Cambodia's freshwater fisheries and degrade agricultural land. If extreme weather conditions damage key infrastructure, tourism and other businesses that depend on it will suffer.

Economic growth and environmental protection are often considered a trade-off. However, they can complement each other, depending on how they are pursued. At the intersection of the two is green growth, where ecologically sustainable economic growth fosters low-carbon but socially inclusive development. Green investment promises to unlock growth potential while creating decent and sustainable jobs for the future.

Cambodia has significant potential to scale up investment in renewable energy and energy efficiency by using its abundant solar energy resources, which are sufficient to absorb more than $900 million in solar photovoltaic investment (UNDP 2019). The Cambodian countryside has many remote villages off the grid. Solar power could provide these often poor communities with affordable, clean energy and thus improve living conditions and economic productivity.

Installed solar capacity has grown very rapidly, from about 20 megawatts (MW) in 2018 to 300 MW in 2020 and 380 MW in 2021. It was expected to increase to 440 MW by 2022, supplying almost 7% of the energy mix (Santos 2022). Hydropower is the largest source of renewable energy in the country, with an installed capacity of 1,330 MW in 2021, representing 44% of the energy mix.

Moving away from heavy reliance on fossil fuels, slowing or arresting deforestation, and adopting more sustainable agricultural and fishing practices are critical for protecting the environment and securing the future prospects of rural industries.

As green and sustainable production becomes increasingly important to businesses and the investment decisions of international firms, it becomes commercially expedient to adopt sustainability standards and thus remain competitive. The upshot is that, by shrinking its carbon footprint and thus responding to global demand for environmentally sustainable products and services, Cambodia could garner new growth opportunities.

These proposals to pursue green growth are consistent with the commitments made by the government through its National Strategic Plan on Green Growth, 2013–2030 and its Long-Term Strategy for Carbon Neutrality by 2050. An update to Cambodia's 2003 Law on Investment in 2022 also reflects this commitment by providing new incentives for businesses deemed to be green: environmental management and protection, biodiversity conservation, the circular economy, and green energy including technology that advances climate change adaptation and mitigation.

(ii) *Financial, Health, and Other Shocks and Crises*

Financial risks. Cambodia will need to strengthen the resilience of its finance sector by improving the regulatory and supervisory framework, improving asset quality and risk management practices, and addressing weaknesses in the banking system. The NBC has taken steps to improve its supervisory capacity and strengthen prudential regulations, but further reforms are needed (IMF 2022; UNCDF 2021). Also important is safeguarding financial stability—particularly in commercial real estate, which has been stressed by the tightening of financial conditions—through measures such as restructuring banks and drafting regulations on corporate insolvency and debt restructuring (World Bank 2022).

To address the growth of shadow banking and the proliferation of nonbank financial institutions, the Non-Bank Financial Services Authority has been established. It will strengthen regulation and supervision, but will take time to become fully operational. The Cambodian authorities also need to accelerate the establishment of a deposit protection scheme, implement measures to prevent money laundering, and clarify the framework for bank resolution (IMF 2021).

The recent acceleration in credit growth has raised concerns about overindebtedness. The Cambodian authorities must therefore carefully monitor the health of banks and MFIs as pandemic-response forbearance measures wind down and be ready to intervene as needed to maintain finance sector stability. Systemically important banks with concentrated exposure to construction and real estate should be monitored particularly closely. A gradual increase in minimum capital requirements could promote consolidation in the banking and microfinance sectors, but would need to be managed carefully.

Health crisis. Government spending on health care is low, keeping Cambodia's health care system capacity one of the lowest in Asia. The country currently has only 0.7 hospital beds per 1,000 people, less than a third of Viet Nam's 2.6 or a sixth of the average of 4.7 in member countries of the Organisation for Economic Co-operation and Development (OECD). This has been a major constraint on managing the COVID-19 pandemic, requiring Cambodia to impose more stringent controls than countries with more robust health care systems. The very low capacity of the health care system was a key factor in the draconian response to the pandemic outbreak in February 2020. Had there been more capacity, the government would have had more breathing space for a more nuanced and targeted approach to managing the outbreak, thereby lightening the burden on the economy and livelihoods.

Given low capacity in the health care system and the high cost imposed by COVID-19 lockdowns, especially for poor people, a hard call for the authorities was how much to try to flatten the curve and where. Access to high-quality health care is much better in urban areas than in rural areas. There is an urgent need to improve both access to and quality of health care in remote areas. Even in urban areas, there is scope to improve the quality of health care. Unless greater investment is made in improving the quality and quantity of health care services, a future pandemic or major public health threat requiring hospitalization could quickly overwhelm the health care system.

(iii) *Technological Change, Especially Acceleration Toward a Digital Economy*

How can Cambodia better manage potential downsides from acceleration toward a digital economy? The willingness to import skills and technology can help countries catch up and address the challenges posed by a digital economy and the Fourth Industrial Revolution in the short term. In the long term, however, these challenges will require a fundamental transformation of education and learning systems. In other words, the digital transition reinforces the need to address the underlying problems of a deficient human capital and skills development, as discussed in Chapter 3.

In addition, governments must implement education reforms that promote lifelong learning so that workers can adapt even late in life to changing conditions and needs. Augmenting cognitive understanding of disciplines such as math and science will be critical for the transition to a more innovative, knowledge-based economy. Regional education networks also need to be strengthened and linked to innovation incubators in the region. New and innovative approaches to public–private collaboration can advance research and development. Preparations for the transition to an economy enabled by knowledge and innovation must begin now so that they can be realized in the medium to long run.

(iv) *Diversifying Export Markets and Import Sources*

Cambodia's trade patterns for both products and markets are heavily influenced by trade preferences. The high share of garments in exports is a function of the Generalized System of Preferences provided by the US and the Everything but Arms preferences provided by the European Union. As Cambodia develops and eventually graduates from LDC status, it will lose preferential access to these markets. As real wages increase with economic development, the garment industry will likely gradually shift to higher value-added products and processes, but not enough to sustain the garment industry's current high share of Cambodia's exports and economy. Even without any deliberate policy to induce diversification, the dominance of the garment industry will diminish with time.

Similarly, any success in addressing major constraints on structural diversification, such as low human capital and high business costs, will alter trade and investment flows. Success in lowering key manufacturing costs, such as for electricity, can attract new types of FDI from new source countries. The composition of exports and imports can change over time, as can the markets and sources. In short, lowering electricity costs can help diversify trade and investment patterns. As such, it is one of several indirect channels through which policy reforms can affect trade and investment patterns.

Nevertheless, specific policy changes can be pursued to diversify trade and investment flows directly. Preferences are laid out in many FTAs to which Cambodia is party, and they skew the product and supplier composition of its imports (ERIA 2021). The margin of preference (MoP), or the difference between preferential treatment and ordinary most favored nation (MFN) status, is still high for many tariff lines and in the various FTAs. For example, Cambodia's average MoP in the ASEAN Trade in Goods Agreement was 13.6% in 2018 (ERIA 2021). High MoPs in various FTAs and tariff lines distort the geographic patterns and composition of imports.

When MoPs are high, trade patterns can be distorted by trade diversion from countries that are not party to an FTA to those that are, often concentrating trade flows. Trade diversion further impinges on welfare by favoring imports that no longer originate from parties that are not the lowest-cost producers. Broader multilateral preferences maximize welfare from trade by minimizing trade diversion, promoting more trade, and enabling more efficient domestic allocation of resources. Therefore, the pursuit of an open region through multilateral FTA preferences is in Cambodia's national interest, as it promotes domestic competitiveness and welfare and alleviates concentrated trade patterns.

What stands in the way of multilateralization in Cambodia and the other newer ASEAN member countries?[10] The reluctance to go beyond the provisions mandated in FTAs and voluntarily extend tariff reductions to nonparties mainly reflects concerns about revenue losses (Lao-Arraya 2002). Although the contribution of trade taxes to government revenue is declining, it remains significant. In 2019, for instance, trade taxes in Cambodia contributed more than 10% to government revenue, compared with 3% in Thailand, 1% in Malaysia, and a global average of 2.4% (Menon 2022b).

Countries that maintain different tariff regimes for each FTA often do so with the expectation that this will reduce revenue losses from participation in FTAs. Is this likely to be true? The revenue impact of such multiple-rate systems compared with a multilateral or single-rate system depends on two factors: administration costs and tariff collection efficiency. In both cases, multilateralization offers better prospects.

First, the cost of administering a multiple-rate system is clearly higher than a single-rate system. To operationalize a multiple-rate system, customs authorities must apply rules of origin to determine the applicable rate. The spread of global supply chains complicates this task, and multiple-rate systems impose higher compliance costs on businesses.

Second, additional tariff revenue is collected only if non-FTA imports are charged higher MFN rates. In multicountry or regional FTAs such as the Regional Comprehensive Economic Partnership there are strong incentives for trade deflection if there is a significant difference between the two rates. Goods from outside the FTA are likely to enter the regional partnership area through a country with a low or zero MFN tariff, such as Singapore, and then be reexported to Cambodia, thereby denying Cambodia the higher tariff revenue.

10 While the original members of ASEAN have embraced an open region through the multilateral application of most of their preferential tariffs under the ASEAN Trade in Goods Agreement and offering them to all countries on an MFN basis, Cambodia and the other newer members of ASEAN have not. Cambodia, the Lao PDR, Myanmar, and Viet Nam have been reluctant to adopt multilateralization, which entails lowering and eventually removing MoPs to end discrimination against trading partners.

Creating a system where multiple rates apply to each tariff line increases the incentives for smuggling and rent-seeking. It is an open secret that the porous borders of the Mekong subregion facilitate illicit trade and that some trade taxes are collected privately rather than on the books.

For these reasons, Cambodia should finally grasp the nettle and pursue multilateralization to enable a less distorted and therefore more diversified trade pattern, make good on open regionalism, and thus reap more of the fruits of globalization.

(v) *Diversifying Sources of Foreign Direct Investment*

As a transition economy and LDC, Cambodia must attract FDI or incur external debt to grow faster than would be possible depending solely on its low domestic savings rate. There is, however, a question of sustainability attached to each of these flows. The need to keep long-term debt sustainable is widely recognized and perhaps better understood than the need to ensure that FDI inflows do not exceed absorptive capacity. FDI sustainability depends on ensuring that the external competitiveness of tradable goods is not impaired by a sharp appreciation of the local currency driven to massive inflows of FDI. This could induce a process of deindustrialization known as the Dutch disease.

As noted in the discussion on prioritizing infrastructure projects, the criteria used by the Council for the Development of Cambodia to vet FDI proposals for QIP status may be incomplete for lack of a comprehensive cost–benefit framework. A formal assessment of the costs and benefits of FDI projects is an essential part of a conventional approval process. A foreign investment review board, as proposed here, could go a long way toward fixing a shortcoming of the current process. A well-functioning review board could help avoid projects that have left the neighboring Lao PDR in severe debt distress. The point is that an economy like Cambodia should be selective in choosing projects, whether they are financed by FDI or by borrowings, to achieve a sustainable and inclusive growth. In addition, increasing the share of new investors can provide Cambodia with access to new markets and global manufacturing supply chains that will support domestic structural change by diversifying sources of growth.

4 Conclusions

Despite its tragic history, Cambodia has great aspirations. It aims to become an upper middle-income country by 2030 and a high-income country by 2050. To achieve these aspirations, Cambodia must pursue inclusive growth that is sustainable and resilient. Such growth should generate decent and sustainable jobs in manufacturing and services, as well as fair and sustainable returns for self-employed people in agriculture or MSMEs in all sectors, whether formal or informal. To achieve this, it must address a number of constraints.

A key constraint that was highlighted in the previous Rectangular Strategy (Phase IV) and the new Pentagon Strategy (Phase I) is the lack of economic diversification. This was also highlighted in the last country diagnostic study (CDS) (ADB 2014), but continues to be a major constraint. The continued lack of diversification has not slowed the rapid pace of economic growth, but only constrained its quality and inclusiveness. Cambodia's rapid growth has been driven by trade preferences, tourism, and large capital inflows for investment in infrastructure and real estate. With LDC graduation expected in this decade, Cambodia will need to pursue new drivers of growth that require greater diversification.

The early phase of diversification or structural transformation, featuring rural–urban migration from agriculture to industry and services, is continuing but may be reaching its limit. This inter-sector transfer of production factors is easy diversification, requiring only minimal government intervention or policy reform as it proceeds under its own steam with minimal adjustment costs. This horizontal shift between sectors toward higher-value products and activities leads to a one-off productivity boost that raises incomes and living standards, but may not be sustainable in the longer term.

Future increases in productivity have to come from intra-sector diversification, or a vertical shift to higher value-added products and activities within the same sector, be it industry, services, or agriculture. This type of diversification—moving up the value chain—usually entails greater participation in global value and supply chains. Unlike in the earlier inter-sector phase of industrialization, this process of upgrading within a sector is unlikely to happen spontaneously, but instead requires government intervention and policy reform.

Two major constraints need to be addressed through policy reforms and government support to enable greater intra-sector diversification. The first is the skills mismatch and inadequate human capital. The second is the high cost of doing business, which constrains private sector development and domestic and foreign investment. Addressing these constraints should make economic growth more inclusive. To give these achievements staying power, other constraints need to be addressed through measures designed to strengthen resilience and sustainability and thus safeguard current and future growth.

To address these constraints, the following policy reforms and government interventions are recommended.

Human Capital

There is an urgent need to improve the quality of education at all levels, not only in tertiary education and TVET, which can only be successful if students have acquired a strong educational foundation in primary and secondary schools. Quality improvements need to be accompanied by measures to raise currently low access and retention rates. When investing in skills development and training, Cambodia needs to collaborate closely with the private sector to avoid skills mismatches. TVET and tertiary education institutions need to align their curricula more closely with the needs of the private sector.

Business Costs

The high cost of doing business in Cambodia stems from the inadequate physical and logistical infrastructure, high energy costs, and high financing costs. Despite notable successes in building infrastructure, a persistent deficit continues to add significantly to business costs. Choke points such as port capacity, logistics infrastructure, and intermodal connectivity should be prioritized.

The high cost of electricity hinders vertical upgrades within electronics and automotive supply chains from labor-intensive assembly to higher value addition through the energy-intensive production of parts and components. Cambodia has significant potential to scale up investment in solar energy and thereby significantly reduce business costs for rural MSMEs off the grid.

Poor access to formal avenues of finance reflects its high cost. The potential for digital innovation through fintech and blockchain presents significant opportunities to improve financial inclusion. Financing costs can be further reduced by tackling corruption and poor governance, strengthening institutions including the legal system, and developing the finance sector and capital markets.

Resilience and Sustainability

Finally, more versatility is needed in managing and responding to disruption and ensuring the sustainability of growth and its drivers. Stronger resilience entails addressing (i) climate change and other environmental pressures; (ii) financial, health, and other shocks or crises; and (iii) technological change, especially acceleration toward a digital economy. Growth and its drivers can be made more sustainable by diversifying trade and investment flows. Diversifying export products and markets and import sources, as well as sources of FDI, will reduce risk and make economic growth more sustainable. Discussion of appropriate policies and interventions follows below.

Addressing Climate Change and Other Environmental Pressures

Climate change threatens the livelihoods of millions of people and Cambodia's long-term aspiration to achieve high-income status by 2050. Economic growth and environmental protection are often considered a trade-off, but they can also complement each other. The intersection between the two is green growth, or ecologically sustainable growth that fosters low-carbon and socially inclusive development. Moving away from heavy reliance on fossil fuels, reducing or arresting deforestation, and adopting more sustainable agricultural and fishing practices are critical for protecting the environment and securing the future prospects of rural industries.

Financial, Health, and Other Shocks or Crises

Financial risks. Cambodia will need to strengthen the resilience of its finance sector by improving the regulatory and supervisory framework, improving asset quality and risk management practices, and addressing weaknesses in the banking system. Regulations must be implemented to deal with corporate insolvency and the restructuring of debt and some banks. The recent rapid pace of credit growth has raised concerns about overindebtedness. As pandemic-induced forbearance measures are phased out, Cambodia's authorities need to carefully monitor the health of banks and MFIs, especially systemically important banks with high exposure to construction and real estate.

Health crisis. While Cambodia managed COVID-19 remarkably well, the pandemic highlighted a number of vulnerabilities in the health care system that need to be addressed before the onset of the next health emergency. Government spending on health care needs to be significantly increased. Cambodia currently has only 0.7 hospital beds per 1,000 people, less than a third of the 2.6 in Viet Nam or a sixth of the average of 4.7 in OECD member countries. This has been a major constraint on managing the COVID-19 pandemic, which has required more stringent controls than in countries with more robust health care systems.

Technological change and the digital economy. The acceleration toward a digital economy has benefits and costs. Many low- and medium-skilled workers may need to be redeployed, requiring substantial reskilling and retraining. Governments must pursue education reforms that promote lifelong learning so that workers can adapt to changing needs and conditions even late in life.

Diversifying export markets and import sources. Cambodia's trade is highly concentrated, both in its products and in its trade partners for exports and imports. This makes the country vulnerable to country- or product-specific external shocks. As Cambodia addresses its major constraints on structural diversification, such as low human capital and high business costs, trade and investment flows will naturally diversify.

The high margins of preference in Cambodia's FTAs skew the product and country composition of imports. The pursuit of an open region through the multilateralization of FTA preferences is in Cambodia's national interest, as it promotes domestic competitiveness and welfare and alleviates concentrated trade patterns.

Diversifying sources of foreign direct investment. Cambodia needs to attract FDI or incur external debt if it is to grow faster than its low domestic savings rate allows. There is, however, a question of sustainability attached to both FDI and debt. The broader macroeconomic impact of FDI proposals needs to be analyzed through a comprehensive cost–benefit framework. A proposed foreign investment review board could fix the shortcomings of the current review process and avoid the kind of projects that have left the Lao PDR in severe debt distress. Cambodia should choose projects selectively, whether they are financed by FDI or borrowings, to achieve sustainable and inclusive growth.

Appendix
Product Space Analysis

In this Appendix, we employ product space analysis, as developed in Hausmann and Klinger (2006) and Hidalgo et al. (2007), to analyze the practical opportunities available to Cambodia to diversify its product mix as part of ongoing structural transformation in pursuit of more inclusive growth. We consider the realistic options available in the short run and in the medium to the long run. To do this, we first analyze Cambodia's current export basket to evaluate how the promotion of high value addition to enable the export of more complex products can improve productive capability and accelerate structural transformation.

Cambodia's current export basket is highly concentrated in products that are rudimentary, or have low economic complexity, as measured by the economic complexity index (ECI).[1] Hausmann and Hidalgo (2011) proposed the ECI to capture an economy's productive knowledge by measuring the complexity of its product mix. Countries with a high ECI tend to produce and export a wide range of more complex products, such as elaborately transformed manufactures and sophisticated services. In contrast, countries with a low ECI generally produce rudimentary products such as unprocessed or lightly processed agricultural commodities, raw materials, and simple and minimally transformed manufactures. The product mix that a country exports can therefore give an indication of its productive capabilities (Figure A1). The evidence suggests that a country's development path is determined by its capacity to accumulate the capabilities required to engage in the high value addition achieved in the manufacture of a variety of complex products.[2]

1 The ECI measures how diversified and complex a country's export basket is and ranks countries accordingly. If a country produces many complex goods, it is generally more economically developed or can expect rapid economic growth. The measures of complexity are based on the method developed by Hidalgo and Hausmann (2009) using information on revealed comparative advantage (RCA) indexes while considering (i) the number of products exported with RCA ≥ 1, and (ii) the number of countries exporting a particular product with RCA ≥ 1.

2 Capabilities are typically thought of as skills, know-how, or tacit knowledge, but can also include physical inputs and other localized attributes such as institutions, culture, and natural amenities. The hypothesis is that countries grow as they acquire new capabilities and learn to combine them to produce complex, high value-added products that require many complementary skills and inputs.

Figure A1: Economic Complexity Indexes for Selected Countries, 1980–2021

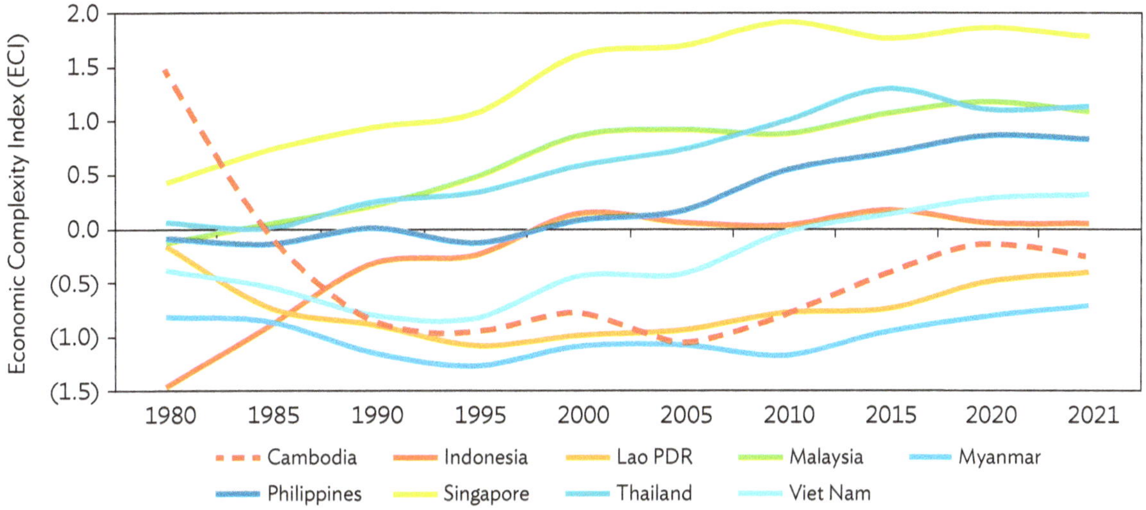

( ) = negative, Lao PDR = Lao People's Democratic Republic.
Source: Computations based on data from the Atlas of Economic Complexity Database. https://dataverse.harvard.edu/dataverse/atlas (accessed 3 July 2024).

An evaluation of Cambodia's product mix shows that the country lags behind most other countries in Southeast Asia, and that its ECI actually declined between 1980 and 2005. Although Cambodia has improved its ECI since 2005, it only outranks the Lao People's Democratic Republic (Lao PDR) and Myanmar in the region. Meanwhile, Indonesia, the Philippines, and Viet Nam have significantly diversified and upgraded their exports, which is reflected in their rising ECI scores. Singapore has the highest ECI in Southeast Asia, reflecting its diverse skills set and higher productive knowledge.

Cambodia's persistently low ECI points to the difficulties the country faces in moving away from low-value products and those with little value added. The stubbornly low ECI suggests that (i) Cambodia's export basket remains dominated by rudimentary products; (ii) the country has not developed the necessary capabilities to move up the value chain or produce new, more sophisticated products; and (iii) it must compete with many other developing countries that export similar products. In other words, Cambodia has yet to acquire the capabilities needed to manufacture complex products with high value added. Its meager product mix suggests that the country will not be able to achieve inclusive growth in the medium to long run (Figure A2).

Figure A2: Economic Complexity and GDP per Capita, 2021

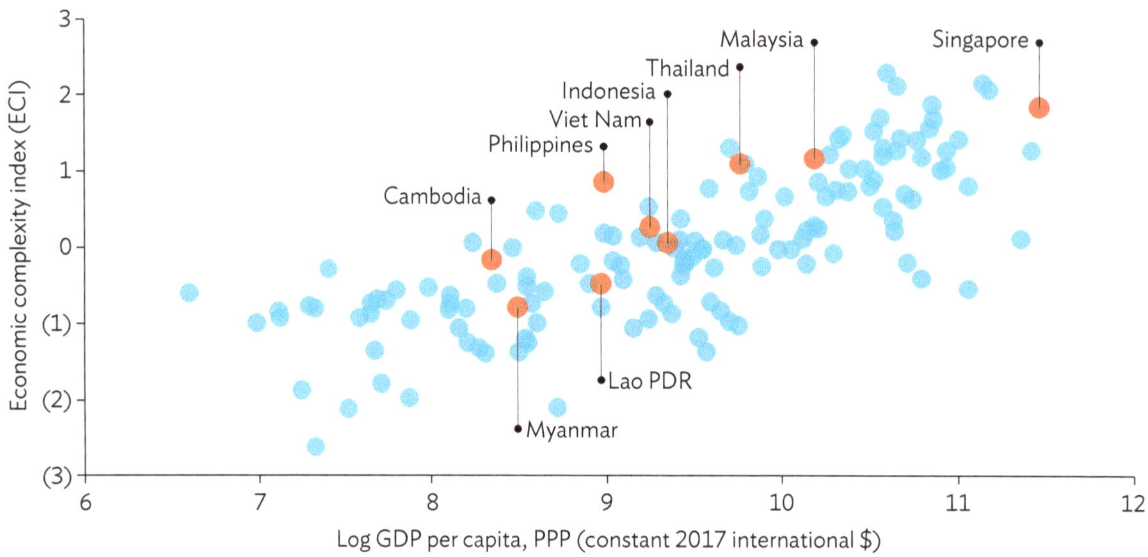

( ) = negative, GDP = gross domestic product, Lao PDR = Lao People's Democratic Republic, PPP = purchasing power parity.
Sources: Estimates based on data from World Bank. World Development Indicators. http://data.worldbank.org/data-catalog/world-developmentindicators; and Atlas of Economic Complexity Database. https://dataverse.harvard.edu/dataverse/atlas (accessed July 2024).

Structural Transformation and Product Space Analysis

The product space methodology is used to identify where opportunities for diversifying the export mix might lie (see box). The global product space is a graphic depiction of the network of connecting products, showing all products exported in the world and how close they are to each other (Hidalgo et al. 2007). The central idea behind the product space is that a country's ability to export a new product depends on its ability to export similar products. Hence, products that require similar capabilities are more likely to be exported together.

Box: Product Space Analysis

Hausmann and Klinger (2006) pioneered product space analysis to analyze structural transformation in an economy. They specifically analyzed a key aspect of structural transformation—product diversification. Further, Hidalgo et al. (2007) mapped products across global economies (box figure). This accounts for proximity by computing the probability of a country having a comparative advantage in one product given its comparative advantage in another. Proximity measures capabilities that are used to produce one product and can be used to produce another. (Capabilities could include knowledge about the product, physical assets, intermediate inputs, labor relations, labor training requirements, technology, marketing, infrastructure, property rights, regulatory requirements, and other public goods.)

continued on next page

Box *continued*

Hidalgo et al. (2007) elaborate using the analogy that the product space is a forest, with trees as the products and monkeys as companies. A monkey can easily jump to "nearby" (proximate) trees, but it needs to exert a gargantuan effort to transfer to "far-away" trees. If the monkey is in the clustered portion of the forest, the monkey has more opportunity to jump from one tree to another. The stock of capabilities accumulated jumping from tree to tree will serve the monkey well. In summary, the capabilities that firms learned in producing several products (diversification) can lead to the development of more high-end products (sophistication).

Hidalgo et al. (2007) measured the distance (proximity) of each pair of products and developed the concept of product space. They applied the network theory to visualize the distance between products by their relative similarities in needed capabilities. Their analysis used an international trade data set based primarily on the Standard International Trade Classification Revision 2, disaggregated at the four-digit level. Data were available for 773 products. The different nodes represent products, and their colors correspond to their product groups based on the Leamer's classification,[a] and the node size is in proportion to world trade values. The colors of the lines that connect the nodes represent the distance between

Product Space

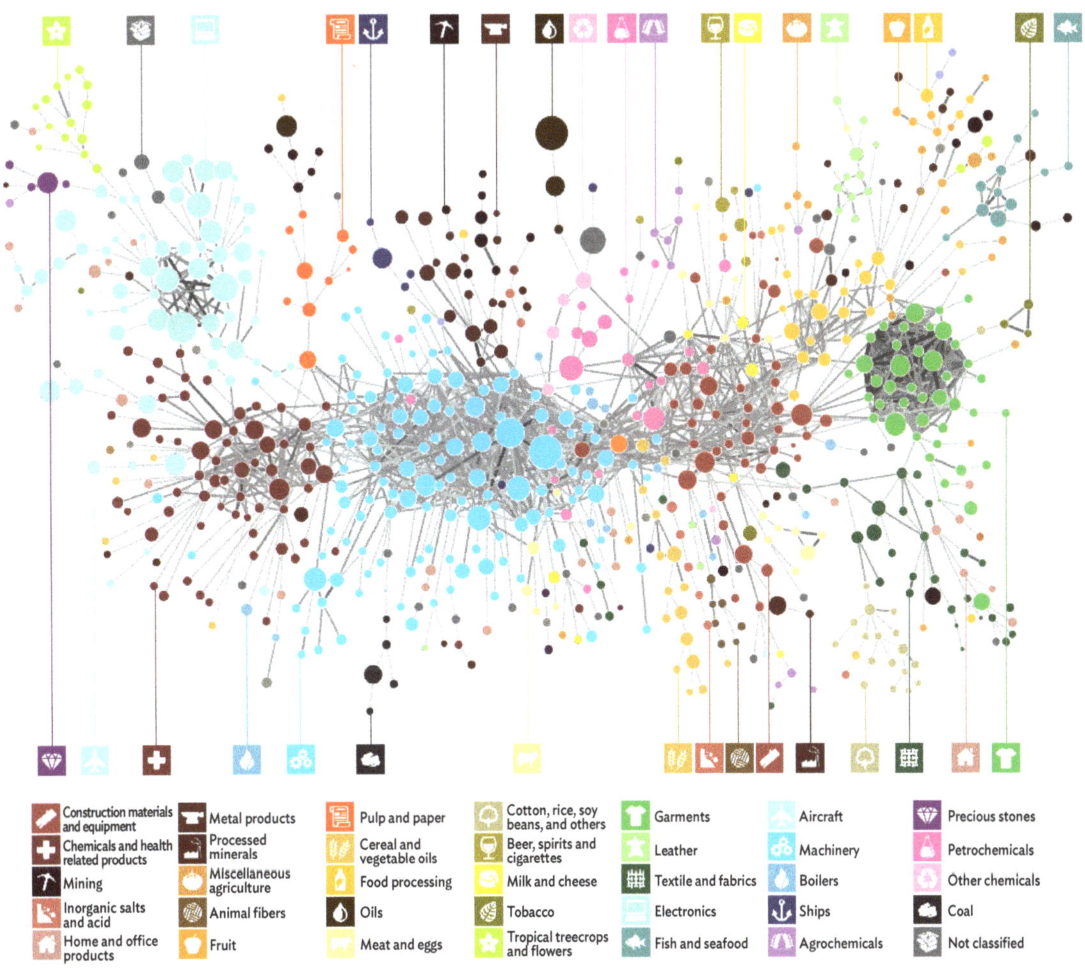

Source: Hidalgo, A. et al. 2007. The Product Space Conditions the Development of Nations. *Science*. 317. pp. 482–487.

continued on next page

Box *continued*

a pair of products. The map is highly heterogeneous, with the dense part representing many products that are closely connected—particularly machinery, chemicals, and capital-intensive products. This indicates the ease with which companies can move from one commodity to another. In the periphery, products such as natural resources, primary products, and agricultural products are weakly connected to others. This indicates the difficulty of moving from these products to other products.

[a] The product classification introduced by Leamer (1984) is based on relative factor intensities, that is, the relative amount of capital, labor, land, or skills required to produce each product.

Sources: Hausmann, R. and B. Klinger. 2006. Structural Transformation and Patterns of Comparative Advantage in the Product Space. CID Working Paper No. 128. Center for International Development, Harvard University; Leamer, E. 1984. Sources of International Comparative Advantage: Theory and Evidence. MIT Press.

Because each product requires unique capabilities and know-how to produce, the product space provides a glimpse into the embedded knowledge that signifies the available productive capabilities and the opportunities that might be feasible. The product space is heterogeneous, with products on the periphery only weakly connected to others, while products in the center are more strongly connected. Typically, products such as agricultural commodities and natural resources are located at the periphery of the product space, indicating that they have little spillover to the rest of the economy.

Therefore, it is difficult for a country that produces and exports such rudimentary products to diversify into more complex, higher value-added products. In contrast, chemicals, machinery, electronics, and transformed metals are generally found in the denser part of the product space. More specifically, less complex products tend to be on the right-hand side of the space, while more complex products tend to be in the central and on the left-hand side of the product space. Developing countries typically diversify and grow their export base starting from the center/right region and gradually move toward the more complex left-hand side (see box).

To achieve structural transformation, countries need to move from sparsely populated, less connected areas of the product space to more dense areas where products are more closely connected. However, such movement requires a more advanced set of capabilities than is available in the sparse areas. As discussed in the main text, Cambodia, having almost exhausted the opportunities of inter-sector diversification through rural–urban migration, currently faces the challenge of achieving intra-sector specialization, which is a more difficult ascent up the value chain. With this kind of diversification, Cambodia would move from the left to the center of the product space. Delaying the next stage of intra-sector diversification would result in Cambodia being stuck in the sparse, left-hand side of the product space, producing products with low and declining income elasticity. This carries a high risk of external demand shocks and worsening terms of trade over time.

Products that require similar capabilities naturally group together in highly connected communities of products. Products within a community are more closely connected with each other than with products outside the community. Moreover, the position of the different communities in the product space matters for structural transformation. The communities that are in the dense part of the product space generally have a more complex set of products with high value or high value added. Other communities that are not well connected tend to have fewer complex products. For example, the products belonging to the machinery community are highly complex and strongly connected. This contrasts sharply with poorly connected communities such as cotton, rice, and petroleum, which tend to be uncomplex. The garments, textile, and food-processing communities are in an intermediate position and are therefore somewhat connected but not very sophisticated. On the other hand, electronics and pharmaceuticals are highly complex, but not as connected as machinery. The capabilities used in their production are thus product-specific, relevant within their communities but not outside of them (Hausmann and Hidalgo 2011).

Empirical evidence suggests that a country's exports influence the rate and quality of economic growth. However, producing new goods is quite different from producing more of the same or similar products. Each product requires highly specific inputs such as knowledge, physical assets, intermediate inputs, labor skills, infrastructure needs, regulatory requirements, and other public goods (Hausmann, Hwang, and Rodrik 2005). This is related in one way or another to the constraints on diversification discussed above and requires both public and private investment to increase the pace of structural transformation.

The discussion underscores the importance of economic diversification and accumulating the capabilities required to produce diverse and complex products with high value added. Thus, a country's position in the product space determines its opportunities to diversify and upgrade its exports.

Next, we analyze Cambodia's product space to assess its achievements and its opportunities to develop the capabilities needed to produce more diverse products (Figure A3).

Figure A3 shows the evolution of the product space in Cambodia from 1980 to 2021. The black squares mark products for which Cambodia has a revealed comparative advantage (RCA) > 1.3. The analysis revealed that Cambodia had 56 products with an RCA > 1 in 1980, but only 30 in 1990, recovering to 56 again in 2000 and rising to 61 in 2010 and 91 in 2021. A more detailed analysis showed that the share of crude materials in all exports was 40.7% in 1980, increasing to 89.4% in 1990, before falling sharply to just 5.3% in 2021. Meanwhile, the export share of garments increased dramatically from 4.5% in 1990 to 79.5% in 2000. It fell to 70.3% in 2010 and further to 47.1% in 2021 but continues to be the largest source of export receipts (Table A1). Cambodia succeeded in increasing the number of products with an RCA > 1 between 1980 and 2021, but most of these products have a low measured level of economic complexity, implying low spillover to the rest of the economy (Table A2).

3 Hidalgo et al. (2007) proposed using the number of products exported with RCA as a measure of diversification. RCA is defined, based on Balassa (1965), as $RCA_{ci} = \frac{xval_{ci} / \sum_i xval_{ci}}{\sum_c xval_{ci} / \sum_{i,c} xval_{ci}}$, where xvalci is the value of the product i exports from country c. A country with RCA > 1 has revealed comparative advantage in that commodity.

Figure A3: Product Space Maps of Cambodia, Selected Years

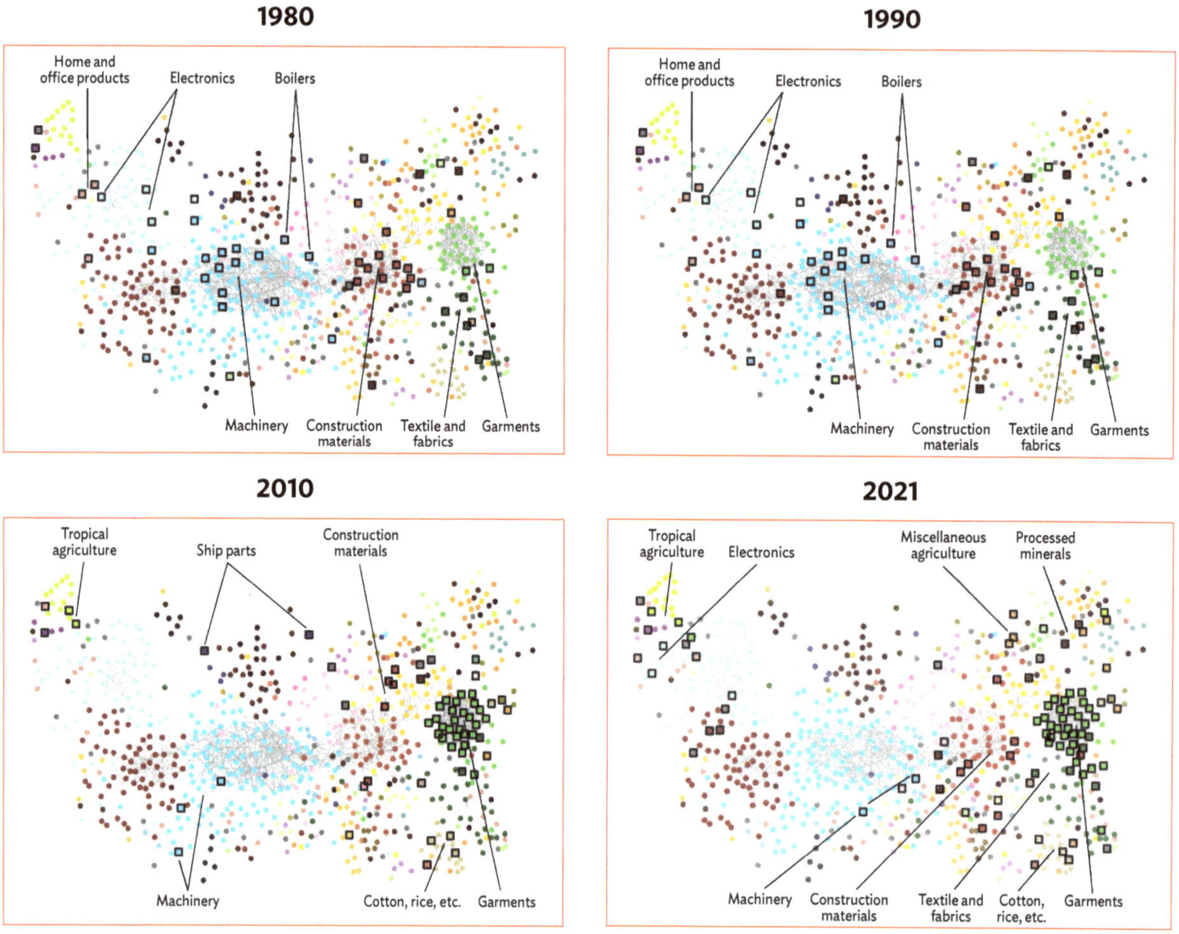

Legend:

Agrochemicals	Cotton, rice, soy beans, and others	Machinery	Petrochemicals
Aircraft	Electronic	Meat and eggs	Precious stones
Animal fibers	Fish and seafood	Metal products	Processed minerals
Beer, spirits, and cigarettes	Food processing	Milk and cheese	Pulp and paper
Boilers	Fruits	Mining	Ships
Cereals and vegetable oils	Garments	Miscellaneous agriculture	Textile and fabrics
Chemicals and health-related products	Home and office products	Not classified	Tobacco
Coal	Inorganic salts and acids	Petroleum	Tropical agriculture
Construction materials and equipment	Leather	Other chemicals	

Source: Computations based on data from the Atlas of Economic Complexity Database. https://dataverse.harvard.edu/dataverse/atlas (accessed 3 July 2024).

Table A1: Number of Products with Revealed Comparative Advantage, 1990–2021

SITC	Commodity	1980 No.	1980 Share (%)	1990 No.	1990 Share (%)	2000 No.	2000 Share (%)	2010 No.	2010 Share (%)	2021 No.	2021 Share (%)
0	Food	0		4	4.40	4	0.84	4	2.28	12	11.22
	Vegetables and fruit	0		0		1	0.10	2	1.31	5	7.56
	Cereals	0		1	1.41	0		2	0.97	3	3.35
	Sugar and honey	0		0		0		0		2	0.19
1	Beverages and tobacco	0		0		0		1	0.10	1	0.02
2	Crude materials	2	40.70	18	89.40	11	5.04	17	6.16	10	5.30
	Crude fertilizer and minerals	0		0		0		2	0.42	3	0.15
	Oilseeds and oleaginous fruit	0		1	6.86	3	0.04	2	0.05	2	0.04
	Mineral fuels	0		0		0		0		0	
3	Animal and vegetable oils	0		0		0		1	0.23	0	
4	Chemical and chemical products	1	0.20	1	0.17	0		0		4	0.23
5	Organic chemicals	0		0		0		0		2	0.15
	Manufactured goods	29	28.70	1	0.16	11	4.16	5	0.57	19	5.37
6	Textile yarn and fabrics	6	3.65	0		6	0.74	4	0.49	8	1.51
	Leather, leather manufactures	2	0.46	0		0		0		6	2.33
	Cork and wood manufactures	3	0.24	0		5	3.42	1	0.08	3	1.16
7	Machinery and transport equip.	15	19.23	2	0.59	2	0.13	5	3.98	5	6.16
	Electric machinery and parts, nes	5	4.56	0		0		0		2	2.72
8	Misc. manufactured articles	9	11.17	4	5.27	27	89.82	27	86.60	39	71.29
	Garments	1	0.18	3	4.50	24	79.46	24	70.34	27	47.05
	Misc. manufactures	5	10.25	1	0.77	1	3.50	1	7.30	7	3.90
	Furniture	0		0		0		0		2	2.15
9	Other manufactured articles	0		0		1	0.01	1	0.08	1	0.40
	TOTAL	**56**	**100.00**	**30**	**100.00**	**56**	**100.00**	**61**	**100.00**	**91**	**100.00**

Misc. = miscellaneous, nes = not elsewhere stated, no. = number of products exported with revealed comparative advantage > 1, SITC = Standard International Trade Classification.

Source: Computations based on data from the Atlas of Economic Complexity Database. https://dataverse.harvard.edu/dataverse/atlas (accessed 3 July 2024).

Table A2: Distribution of Product Complexity and Export Share, 2021
(%)

SITC	Commodity	Average PCI Rank	Product Complexity Level (1 = highest, 6 = lowest)						
			1	2	3	4	5	6	Total
0	Food	707			0.00	0.24	1.69	9.13	11.06
	Vegetables and fruit	725					0.22	7.12	7.34
	Cereals	682			0.00	0.04	1.46	1.65	3.15
	Sugar and honey	677				0.01	0.00	0.18	0.18
1	Beverages and tobacco	625			0.00	0.01	0.05	0.03	0.09
2	Crude materials	708	0.00	0.00	0.13	0.12	0.84	4.60	5.69
	Crude fertilizer and minerals	680				0.00	0.01	0.13	0.14
	Oilseeds and oleaginous fruit	739						0.12	0.12
3	Mineral fuels	572					0.00		0.00
4	Animal and vegetable oils	729			0.00		0.01	0.08	0.09
5	Chemical and chemical products	227	0.22	0.18	0.06	0.10	0.01	0.00	0.58
	Organic chemicals	137	0.18	0.10	0.00				0.28
6	Manufactured goods	481	0.28	0.57	0.48	2.40	2.10	0.88	6.71
	Textile yarn and fabrics	540	0.20	0.02	0.00	0.09	0.92	0.36	1.59
	Leather, leather manufactures	457			0.22	1.79	0.10	0.08	2.20
	Cork and wood manufactures	555			0.07	0.14	0.98		1.19
7	Machinery and transport equipment	274	2.26	0.99	2.94	1.56	0.01	0.03	7.79
	Electric machinery and parts, nes	266	1.56	0.28	0.18	1.56			3.58
8	Misc. manufactured articles	569	0.06	2.75	4.14	9.08	26.28	24.62	66.92
	Garments	634				0.29	18.82	24.52	43.63
	Misc. manufactures	330	0.00	1.55	2.13	0.33	0.08	0.09	4.19
	Furniture	327			1.99	0.12			2.11
9	Other manufactured articles	650		0.00	0.00	0.19	0.38	0.50	1.07
	TOTAL	**748**	**2.82**	**4.50**	**7.76**	**13.69**	**31.36**	**39.87**	**100.00**

PCI = product complexity index, SITC = Standard International Trade Classification.
Note: Product complexity is based on the PCI ranking, whereby the products are grouped into six levels. Level 1 consists of products with PCI rank 1–128, level 2 of products with rank 128–256, level 3 of products with rank 257–384, level 4 of products with rank 385–512, level 5 of products with rank 513–640, and level 6 of products with rank 641–766. Level 1 contains products with the highest value added, while level 6 has the lowest.
Source: Computations based on data from the Atlas of Economic Complexity Database. https://dataverse.harvard.edu/dataverse/atlas (accessed 3 July 2024).

While Cambodia expanded its products with comparative advantage from 1980 to 2021 and started exporting 91 new products with RCA > 1, most of the new products had low value added, and all exports generated an export value per capita of only $1,177 (Figure A4). This performance compares poorly with other Southeast Asian countries, as Malaysia was able to export 137 products with RCA > 1 and generate an export value per capita of $7,021. Similarly, Thailand exported 223 products and generated an export value per capita of $3,779, and Viet Nam exported 161 new products and an export value per capita of $3,450.

Figure A4: Products with Comparative Advantage and Exports per Capita for Selected Countries, 2021

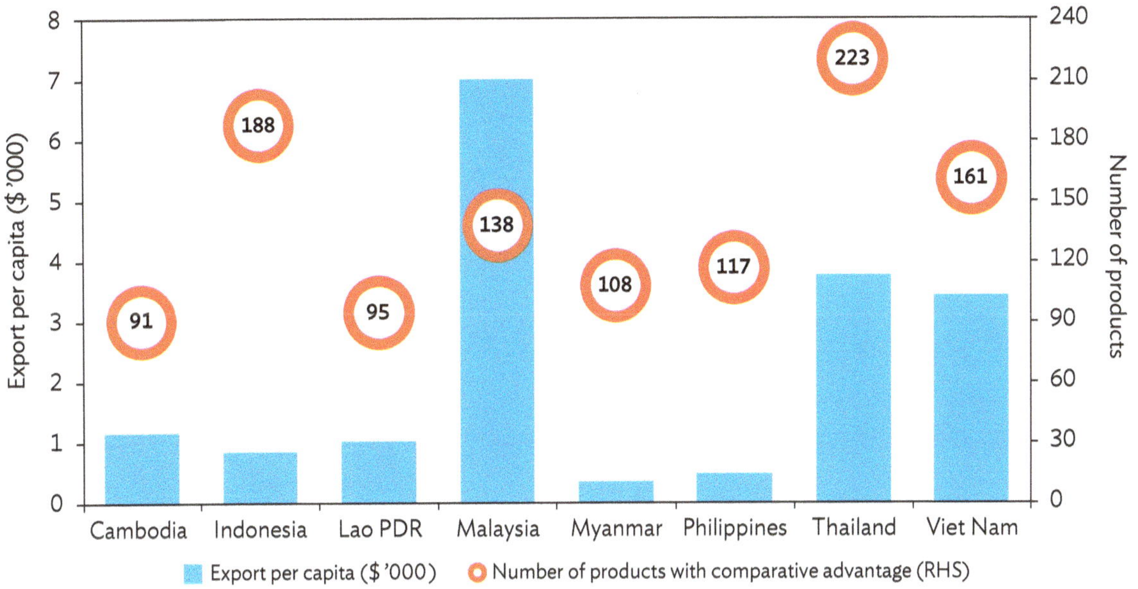

Lao PDR = Lao People's Democratic Republic, RHS = right-hand scale.
Source: Computations based on data from the Atlas of Economic Complexity Database. https://dataverse.harvard.edu/dataverse/atlas (accessed 3 July 2024).

A more disaggregated analysis shows that although Cambodia had exported 91 products with an RCA > 1, their average rank on the product complexity index remained low. Only six of the 91 products exported in 1980 increased their export volume from 1980 to 2021. The overall product complexity rank of these 6 classic products is estimated at 576 out of 765 products, indicating their low value or value added (Table A3).

Table A3: Communities of Products (RCA > 1) in Cambodia, 1980–2021

Community	No. of Products	Average PCI Rank	Cambodia Exports ($ million)	World Exports ($ million)
A. Classic Products				
Garments	1	621	551.6	27,185.0
Construction materials and equipment	1	448	400.6	135,854.4
Not classified	1	742	24.4	16,843.0
Textile and fabrics	1	627	19.3	5,070.7
Processed minerals	1	696	21.8	7,572.3
Home and office products	1	499	7.8	4,711.6
Subtotal (A)	**6**	**576**	**1,025.5**	**197,237.0**

continued on next page

Table A3 *continued*

Community	No. of Products	Average PCI Rank	Cambodia Exports ($ million)	World Exports ($ million)
B. Emerging Products				
(i) Expanding comparative advantage in existing communities				
Garments	32	600	14,828.3	745,967.7
Construction materials and equipment	7	418	823.8	243,716.9
Not classified	6	507	178.6	18,687.9
Textile and fabrics	4	606	246.2	88,214.2
Processed minerals	3	484	229.1	89,214.5
Home and office products	2	370	693.4	15,629.9
(ii) Comparative advantage in new communities				
Miscellaneous agriculture	8	693	707.9	42,207.5
Cotton, rice, soybeans, and others	4	718	1,787.9	60,131.1
Tropical agriculture	3	752	1,225.7	37,392.1
Electronics	3	250	989.3	301,108.7
Machinery	2	189	170.5	74,809.2
Leather	2	664	13.6	1,585.8
Other chemicals	2	234	439.3	178,738.0
Chemicals and health-related products	2	194	34.7	26,899.0
Precious stones	1	747	6.1	1,072.9
Tobacco	1	719	6.0	1,804.3
Meat and eggs	1	453	459.1	1,435.2
Mining	1	490	18.5	7,525.3
Inorganic salts and acids	1	539	3.2	2,143.1
Subtotal (B)	**85**	**557**	**22,861.2**	**1,938,283.3**
TOTAL (A + B)	**91**	**575**	**23,886.7**	**2,135,520.3**

PCI = product complexity index, RCA = revealed comparative advantage.
Source: Computations based on data from the Atlas of Economic Complexity Database. https://dataverse.harvard.edu/dataverse/atlas (accessed 3 July 2024).

The analysis thus underscores the importance of developing capabilities needed to upgrade production and diversify exports. So far, Cambodia has been able to acquire certain capabilities by expanding exports of its traditional products, but these capabilities cannot be used to produce a diverse set of complex products. In other words, Cambodia has yet to expand its productive knowledge sufficiently to produce complex products with high value added. Consequently, despite high economic growth, most of the labor force has remained in low-productivity sectors, stalling the progress on structural change that would support more inclusive growth.

How Cambodia Can Diversify and Upgrade Its Exports

The analysis in this chapter examines what realistic opportunities Cambodia has to diversify and upgrade its exports. To support broader-based and more inclusive growth, Cambodia needs to diversify its exports. It should expand its investments in products that (i) have higher product complexity, (ii) require capabilities nearer at hand, and (iii) offer high opportunity gain.[4]

As mentioned earlier, product complexity is measured using the product complexity index, and distance refers to how far the know-how or capabilities needed to produce other products are from Cambodia's existing capabilities. The opportunity gain index assesses the ability of a new product to open the door to producing more complex products. A high positive value on the opportunity gain index indicates that the product is linked to many other products in terms of its capabilities. However, not all products offer the best avenue for diversifying and upgrading the export basket, and often these three desired properties pose trade-offs. Products that are complex require a large variety of capabilities. Such products tend to be farthest from existing productive knowledge. Similarly, products that offer higher opportunity gain and the best prospects for diversification tend to lie far away.

Next, we analyze the opportunities available to Cambodia that would diversify and upgrade its export basket, given the existing productive knowledge. To identify the unexploited products that would increase the complexity of the economy and therefore create a more diverse and attractive product mix, we look at the number of products exported by all countries in the world. We use an international trade data set based primarily on the Standard International Trade Classification (SITC) Revision 2, disaggregated to four digits. Of the 765 suggested products, we eliminate the 91 where Cambodia had comparative advantage in 2021, leaving 674 products. We also remove products not exported by Cambodia in 2021 (246), leaving 428 products. Wood products, fur clothing, unclassified transactions, artworks, and armored vehicles, firearms and ammunition (13) have also been excluded, leaving 415 products. These 415 are the unexploited products, which we then map to find their distance and product complexity, as well as distance and opportunity gain (Figure A5).

4 Opportunity gain measures how well positioned a country is in the product space by calculating the country's distance from products that it does not currently export with comparative advantage, weighted by the complexity value of each product (Hausmann and Hidalgo 2011).

Figure A5: The Basic Trade-Off Between Distance, Product Complexity, and Opportunity Gain, 2021

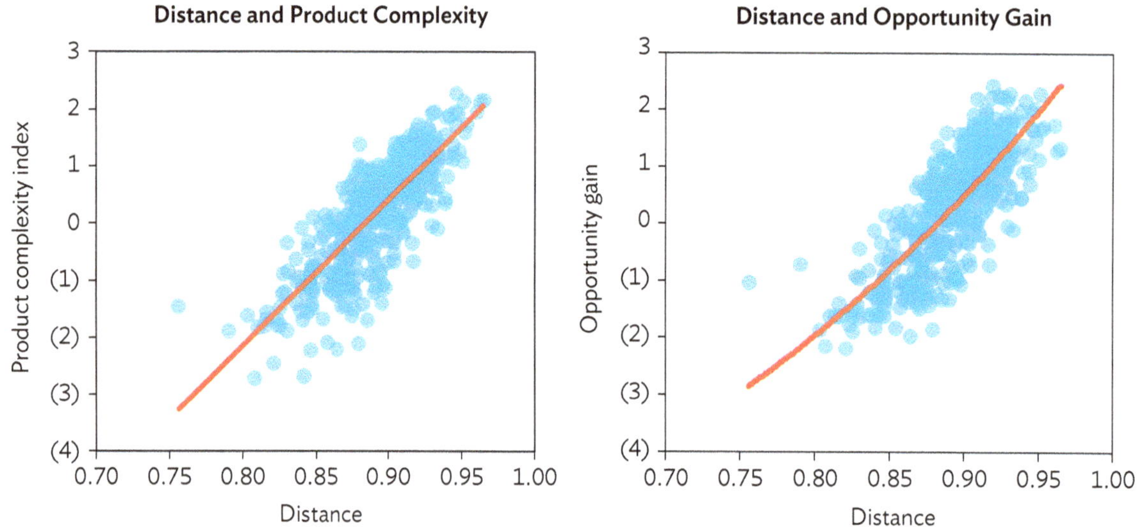

Source: Computations based on data from the Atlas of Economic Complexity Database. https://dataverse.harvard.edu/dataverse/atlas (accessed 3 July 2024).

These unexploited products can further be grouped into nearby, middle-distance, and far-away categories. Products that require inputs and endowments that Cambodia already possesses are the nearby products, or low-hanging fruit. Products requiring somewhat different and more advanced capabilities and know-how are classified as middle-distance products, and those that require rather more advanced capabilities are far-away products. When considering higher investment into unexploited products, entrepreneurs should invest initially in nearby products. Then, as they acquire more advanced capabilities, they should expand investment into some of the middle-distance and far-away products.

It is noteworthy that, while it is relatively easy to expand investment into nearby products, doing so brings only modest improvement in income and diversification of the export basket. Such nearby products offer little spillover and are insufficient to accelerate structural transformation. In the long run, it is the middle-distance and far-away products that should be targeted. Further, capabilities in the production of these products with high value added can be redeployed to other, similar products, thereby creating the synergies and network effects necessary to attract entrepreneurs to invest in other promising but unexploited products. A move from current capabilities to middle-distance and far-away products that look like good strategic bets will succeed only if constraints on human capital and business costs are addressed. In this way, the private sector can be engaged and encouraged to invest in these opportunities and thus accelerate structural transformation for more inclusive growth.

We map in Figure A6 all these unexploited and relatively complex products whose inclusion can help to improve the overall complexity. The horizontal line in Figure A6 reflects the average complexity of Cambodia's current export basket. Since all products above this line are more complex than Cambodia's current exports, expanding investment in these unexploited products may improve the quality and diversity of exports.

Figure A6: Unexploited Export Products of Cambodia, 2021

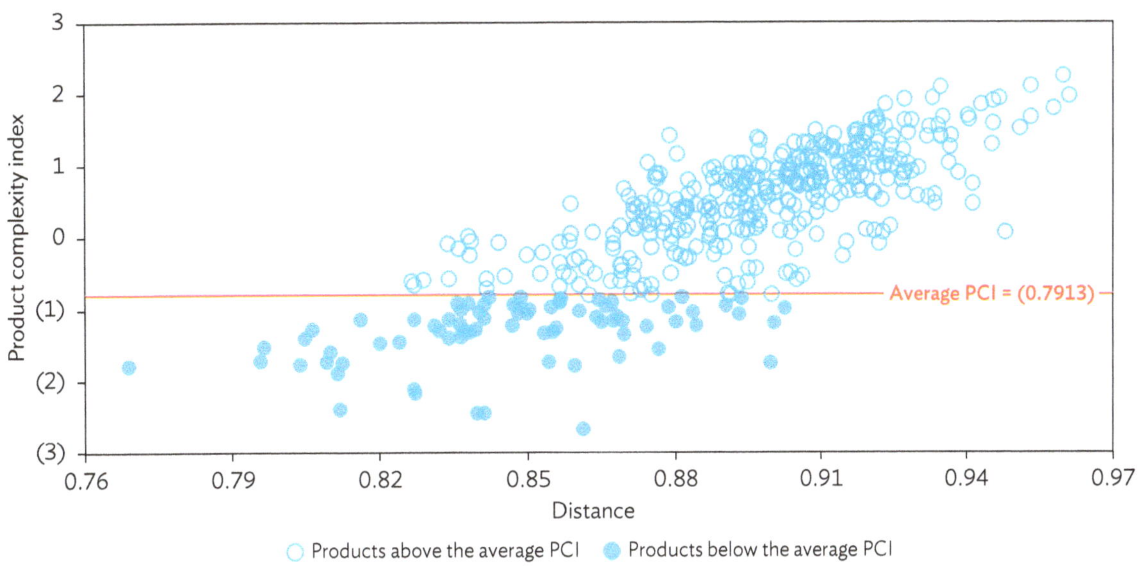

PCI = product complexity index.
Source: Computations based on data from the Atlas of Economic Complexity Database. https://dataverse.harvard.edu/dataverse/atlas (accessed 3 July 2024).

Since all of these unexploited products require advanced capabilities, we can further classify them according to their distance from the current capabilities of Cambodia's labor force and entrepreneurs. For this purpose, a vertical line describing the current average distance is inserted in Figure A7. This helps to divide these unexploited products into two distinct categories: frontier products and far-away products. The frontier products can be thought of as a combination of the nearby and middle-distance products already described earlier, which are promising candidates for short-term diversification. The far-away products are more complex and require training, skills, and inputs that the private sector may not have within reach. The government would need to work closely with the private sector to identify the product-specific constraints and provide the necessary incentives and missing public inputs to make such investments viable in the medium to long run.

Figure A7: Frontier Products of Cambodia, 2021

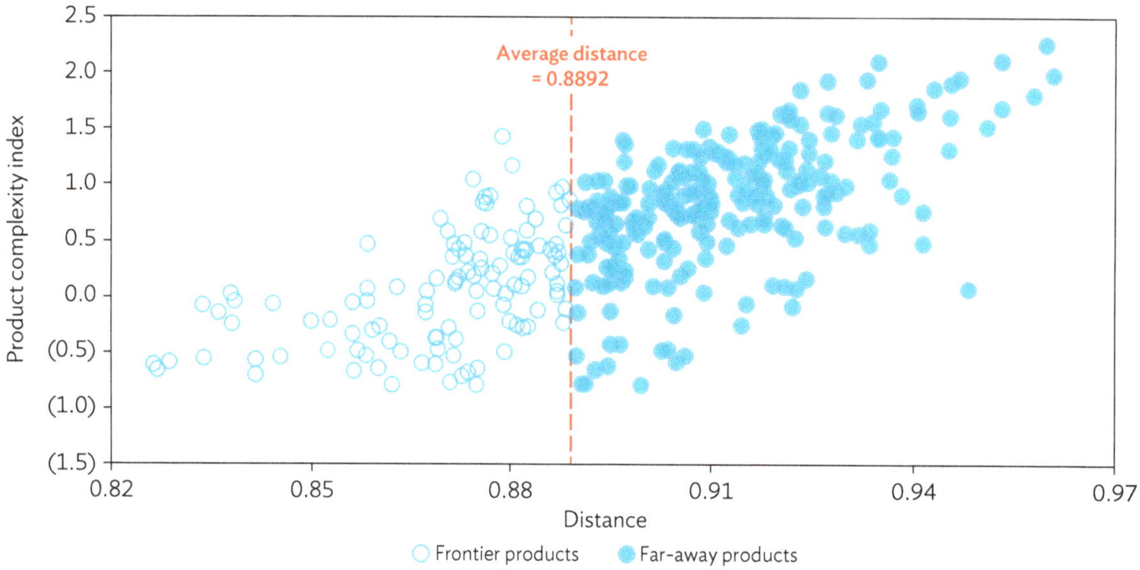

() = negative.
Note: The only unexploited products considered are those that Cambodia is already exporting.
Source: Computations based on data from the Atlas of Economic Complexity Database. https://dataverse.harvard.edu/dataverse/atlas (accessed 3 July 2024).

To identify products with high potential, we classify frontier products as those that are no further from the mean than a 1.5 standard deviation. They are listed in Table A4, along with their complexity index, current export value, and opportunity gain index, as well as the demand for them in regional and global markets. These products are more complex and are good possibilities nearby for future diversification. It must be emphasized that the data-driven approach is not meant to "pick winners," but rather should be viewed as an initial step in identifying potential areas for investment. This also provides to the government a platform on which to design policies for education and training and engage private entrepreneurs in a meaningful dialogue to ascertain product-specific constraints.

As can be seen in Table A4, this data-driven approach identifies five products that are relatively close to Cambodia's current capabilities. Expanding exports of these products can open up new opportunities and improve prospects for sustainable, more inclusive growth. As these products are more complex, expanding investment in these unexploited opportunities can contribute to increased structural transformation.

It is noteworthy that Cambodia is already exporting these products despite not having a revealed comparative advantage in these areas. By producing and processing these products, entrepreneurs have already acquired important capabilities that they can use to venture even further into opportunities with high potential—if conditions are right and the environment is conducive. To induce private investment in these areas, the government needs to work closely with the private sector to overcome the critical constraints on human capital and business costs, as identified above. This analysis suggests that nearby products in forestry, textiles, and printing services offer opportunities to expand investment in the short run (Table A4).

Table A4: Option 1—Nearby Frontier Products, 1.5 Standard Deviation Below Mean Distance, 2021

ISIC	ISIC Description	No	SITC	SITC Description	PCI Rank	Opportunity Gain Rank	Cambodia Exports ($ '000)	World Exports ($ billion)	Regional Imports ($ million)
171	Textiles	1	6514	Non-retail synthetic yarn	433	420	3,701	26.9	2,990.4
		2	6531	Synthetic woven fabrics	542	521	1,532	29.8	6,272.2
		3	6574	Elastic fabrics	410	394	206	1.3	262.3
172	Other textiles	4	6549	Misc. woven fabrics	538	511	267	0.3	39.8
		5	6560	Embroidery	423	407	6,034	8.2	1,432.7
210	Paper products	6	6575	Ropes and cables	552	550	4,396	6.0	743.4
222	Printing services	7	6423	Notebooks	530	527	1,482	4.2	137.3
269	Nonmetallic mineral products n.e.c.	8	6664	Porcelain	465	428	120	7.2	685.7
331	Medical appliances	9	8212	Medical furniture	447	436	30,844	27.3	994.5

ISIC = International Standard Industrial Classification, misc. = miscellaneous, n.e.c. = not elsewhere classified, PCI = product complexity index, RCA = revealed comparative advantage, SITC = Standard International Trade Classification.

Notes:

(i) The analysis shows only those products that have a positive opportunity gain. A positive and higher value of the opportunity gain index indicates that the product links to a larger number of products in terms of capabilities.

(ii) The table shows all unexploited products (RCA < 1) of Cambodia in 2020, excluding (i) products whose PCI is below the average PCI; (ii) garments, works of art, special transactions, and military equipment; (iii) products that have no export value; and (iv) products with a distance that equals to or less than 1.5 standard deviation above the mean for all unexploited products. The remaining products meeting the above criteria were combined into ISIC Revision 3 sectors and weighted by 2018 world exports.

Source: Computations based on data from the Atlas of Economic Complexity Database. https://dataverse.harvard.edu/dataverse/atlas (accessed 3 July 2024).

The analysis shows that Cambodia's current exports of these nearby products are rather lower than the demand for them in regional and global markets. While these nearby products are likely candidates for new investment, this type of diversification would have minimal spillover effects that would benefit the rest of the economy. Therefore, in the long term, products with even greater distance and that require more advanced capabilities should be targeted. The middle-distance and far-away products have the potential to raise income per capita more and generate greater spillover effects to the rest of the economy. Hence, investing in them may be important to promote the desired more inclusive type of structural transformation.

To identify more complex products that are currently at a greater distance from Cambodia's current capabilities, the analysis is repeated, with the distance further decreased from 1.5 to 1.0 standard deviation. This reduction in the capabilities distance yields an additional 10 products with high value added (Table A5). These would have higher spillover into the rest of the economy and could induce more investment in closely related products through agglomeration and network effects. Producing these products would require more advanced skill sets and know-how and greater attention to the full range of business costs that currently inhibit such investment.

Table A5: Option 2—Middle-Distance Products, 1.0 Standard Deviation from Mean Distance, 2021

ISIC	ISIC Description	No	SITC	SITC Description	PCI Rank	Opportunity Gain Rank	Cambodia Exports ($ '000)	World Exports ($ billion)	Regional Imports ($ million)
011	Crop farming	1	2926	Live plants	554	543	47.4	13.9	192.9
151	Food processing	2	0565	Vegetables	559	555	97.9	19.8	857.0
		3	0586	Temporarily preserved fruit	525	516	2,716.1	7.4	129.9
155	Beverages	4	1110	Misc. beverages	482	465	631.9	29.4	1,747.5
171	Textiles	5	6538	Fabrics <85% continuous reg. fibers	512	481	48.9	1.5	217.3
173	Knitted and crocheted fabrics	6	6553	Elastic knitted fibers	462	440	6,958.7	9.5	2,967.5
210	Paper products	7	6421	Paper office containers	456	451	21,663.4	29.5	1,776.7
269	Nonmetallic mineral products	8	6666	Misc. ceramic ornaments	430	406	195.3	2.8	149.2
		9	8122	Ceramic fixtures	534	503	2.1	11.9	1,543.2
369	Other manufacturing	10	8993	Candles and matches	427	417	1,554.8	7.8	242.2

ISIC = International Standard Industrial Classification, Misc. = miscellaneous, n.e.c. = not elsewhere classified, PCI = product complexity index, RCA = revealed comparative advantage, SITC = Standard International Trade Classification.
Notes: The table shows all unexploited products (RCA < 1) of Cambodia in 2019, excluding (i) products whose PCI is below the average PCI; (ii) garments, works of art, special transactions, and military equipment; (iii) products that have no export value; and (iv) products with a distance that is less than 1.0 standard deviation above the mean for all unexploited products. The remaining products meeting the above criteria were combined into ISIC Revision 3 sectors and weighted by 2018 world exports.
Source: Computations based on data from the Atlas of Economic Complexity Database. https://dataverse.harvard.edu/dataverse/atlas (accessed 3 July 2024).

The analysis indicates that these additional products with high potential can broadly be grouped into the following ISIC categories:

(i) crop farming,
(ii) food processing,
(iii) beverages,
(iv) textiles,
(v) knitted and crocheted fabrics,
(vi) paper products,
(vii) nonmetallic mineral products, and
(viii) other manufacturing.

Finally, we repeat the analysis by reducing the distance from 1.0 to 0.5 standard deviation from the mean. This allows us to identify 34 additional opportunities to expand investment in the long run. These products have an even higher opportunity gain that could significantly increase incomes through structural transformation (Table A6).

Table A6: Option 3—More Middle-Distance Products, 0.5 Standard Deviation from Mean Distance, 2021

ISIC	ISIC Description	SITC	SITC Description	PCI Rank	Opportunity Gain Rank	Cambodia Exports ($ '000)	World Exports ($ billion)	Regional Imports ($ million)
141	Quarrying: stone, sand and clay	2734	Stones	472	455	1.1	3.5	193.1
142	Mining and quarrying n.e.c.	2786	Metal waste	477	459	55.3	2.1	273.7
151	Food processing	0583	Fruit jams	516	515	28.7	3.7	110.9
		4235	Olive oil	541	477	927.1	8.9	84.5
		4249	Fixed vegetable oils	568	554	11.6	3.7	175.1
153	Grain mill products	0481	Misc. cereal grains	506	508	13.0	8.0	303.6
154	Other food products	0484	Baked goods	449	438	10,080.7	42.4	1,474.3
		0620	Confectionary sugar	485	473	654.8	12.7	516.0
		0712	Coffee extracts	487	484	4.2	7.6	1,100.6
160	Tobacco products	1223	Tobacco substitutes	523	518	1,999.3	10.7	241.4
171	Textiles	2613	Raw silk	574	480	15.5	0.3	16.9
		6517	Yarn of regenerated fibers	424	408	218.9	2.9	161.7
		6536	Fabrics >85% discon. reg. fibers	360	365	135.4	2.7	320.4
172	Other textiles	6595	Misc. human-made carpets	492	468	7.8	10.9	293.0
		6596	Misc. carpets	510	502	3.8	4.4	222.5
191	Leather products	6129	Misc. articles of leather	397	377	1,746.2	2.8	221.4
210	Paper products	6428	Misc. articles of paper	431	421	9,939.6	34.0	2,206.0
243	Human-made fibers	2665	Uncarded discon. synthetic fibers	297	266	4,771.8	7.9	828.5
252	Plastics products	8931	Plastic storage containers	404	382	73,310.7	64.1	4,152.4
271	Basic iron and steel	6725	Iron billets	563	522	9,011.5	52.0	5,170.6
		6732	Iron bars and rods	543	531	724.6	46.6	3,679.8
		6770	Uninsulated steel wire	388	368	7.0	16.0	1,855.3
		6783	Misc. iron tubes and pipes	478	464	5,857.2	34.1	2,584.5
281	Structural metal products	6912	Aluminum structures	286	244	350.0	15.5	841.6
		6924	Metal containers	372	345	11,508.1	18.9	994.6
289	Fabricated metal products	6931	Metal cables	366	341	254.8	11.6	1,054.9
		6974	Misc. dom. articles, base metals	486	460	20,730.1	25.2	1,887.3
		6978	Misc. base metal HH appliances	549	490	897.5	4.0	157.0
292	Special purpose machinery	7243	Sewing machinery	258	273	2,730.0	6.0	1,055.7
293	Domestic appliances n.e.c.	6973	Domestic nonelectric stoves	375	354	1,875.4	19.9	557.8

continued on next page

Table A6 *continued*

ISIC	ISIC Description	SITC	SITC Description	PCI Rank	Opportunity Gain Rank	Cambodia Exports ($ '000)	World Exports ($ billion)	Regional Imports ($ million)
323	Television and radio receivers, etc.	7611	Color TVs	313	301	563.5	86.4	4,573.5
		7642	Audio amplifiers	224	307	267.6	27.9	2,416.4
351	Ships and boats	7932	Ships and boats	519	494	3,326.1	85.8	7,698.9
369	Other manufacturing	8947	Sporting goods	283	300	56,081.8	49.3	1,915.3

discon. = discontinuous, ISIC = International Standard Industrial Classification, HH = household, misc. = miscellaneous, n.e.c. = not elsewhere classified, PCI = product complexity index, RCA = revealed comparative advantage, SITC = Standard International Trade Classification.

Notes: The table shows all unexploited products (RCA < 1) of Cambodia in 2019, excluding (i) products whose PCI is below the average PCI; (ii) garments, works of art, special transactions, and military equipment; (iii) products that have no export value; and (iv) products with a distance that is less than 0.5 standard deviation above the mean for all unexploited products. The remaining products meeting the above criteria were combined into ISIC Revision 3 sectors and weighted by 2018 world exports.

Source: Computations based on data from the Atlas of Economic Complexity Database. https://dataverse.harvard.edu/dataverse/atlas (accessed 3 July 2024).

These additional products can be grouped into the following broad categories:

(i) mining and quarrying;
(ii) food processing;
(iii) grain mill and other products;
(iv) tobacco products;
(v) textiles and leather products;
(vi) paper and plastic products;
(vii) human-made fibers;
(viii) metal products;
(ix) advanced machinery products
(x) domestic appliances;
(xi) television and radio receivers;
(xii) ships and boats; and
(xiii) other manufacturing.

The foregoing discussion suggests that Cambodia has many interesting opportunities to expand investments that would diversify and upgrade its export basket in the short, medium, and long run. That current exports in these unexploited products are quite low, despite high demand in regional and global markets, suggests great potential for expanding private investment to promote diversification. But first, constraints on structural transformation, particularly human capital and business costs, need to be addressed in a timely manner.

References

Amarthalingam, S. 2020. Keeping It Riel, Cambodia Steps Up De-dollarisation. *Phom Penh Post*. 25 June. https://www.phnompenhpost.com/special-reports/keeping-it-riel-cambodia-steps-de-dollarisation.

Asian Development Bank (ADB). 2014. *Country Diagnostic Study: Cambodia, Diversifying beyond Garments and Tourism*. https://www.adb.org/sites/default/files/publication/149852/cambodia-diversifying-country-diagnostic-study.pdf.

———. 2021. *Cambodia Agriculture, Natural Resources, and Rural Development Sector Assessment, Strategy, and Road Map*. https://www.adb.org/sites/default/files/publication/718806/cambodia-agriculture-rural-development-road-map.pdf.

———. 2023a. *Completion Report: COVID-19 Active Response and Expenditure Support Program*. https://www.adb.org/sites/default/files/project-documents/54195/54195-001-pcr-en.pdf.

———. 2023b. *Asian Development Outlook, April 2023*. https://www.adb.org/publications/asian-development-outlook-april-2023.

Balassa, B. 1965. Trade Liberalization and Revealed Comparative Advantage. *Manchester School*. 33 (2). pp. 99–123. https://doi.org/10.1111/j.1467-9957.1965.tb00050.x.

Cartas, J. M. 2010. Dollarization Declines in Latin America. *Finance & Development*. 47 (1). International Monetary Fund. https://www.imf.org/external/pubs/ft/fandd/2010/03/dataspot.htm.

Chheang, V. 2021. BRI Projects in Cambodia and Laos Roll on Despite Covid-19. *Perspective*. 2021 (99). ISEAS-Yusuf Ishak Institute. https://www.iseas.edu.sg/wp-content/uploads/2021/07/ISEAS_Perspective_2021_99.pdf.

Economic Research Institute for ASEAN and East Asia. 2021. *Impact of the ASEAN Trade in Goods Agreements (ATIGA) on Inter-ASEAN Trade*. Economic Research Institute for ASEAN+3. Chapter 5. https://www.eria.org/publications/impact-of-the-asean-trade-in-goods-agreements-atiga-on-intra-asean-trade/.

Fischer, S. 2006. *Dollarization*. Keynote address to the 75th Anniversary Conference of the Central Bank of the Republic of Turkey. Istanbul. 13–15 December. https://www.bis.org/review/r061221e.pdf.

García-Escribano, M. and S. Sosa. 2011. What Is Driving Financial De-Dollarization in Latin America. *IMF Working Paper*. 11/10. International Monetary Fund. https://www.imf.org/external/pubs/ft/wp/2011/wp1110.pdf.

Hausmann, R. and C. Hidalgo. 2011. The Network Structure of Economic Output. *Journal of Economic Growth*. 16 (4). pp. 309–342. doi:10.1007/s10887-011-9071-4.

Hausmann, R., J. Hwang, and D. Rodrik. 2005. What You Export Matters. *Working Paper*. 11905. National Bureau of Economic Research. https://www.nber.org/system/files/working_papers/w11905/w11905.pdf.

Hausmann, R. and B. Klinger. 2006. Structural Transformation and Patterns of Comparative Advantage in the Product Space. *CID Working Paper*. No. 128. Center for International Development, Harvard University.

Herrendorf, B., R. Rogerson, and Á. Valentinyi. 2013. Growth and Structural Transformation. *NBER Working Paper*. 18996. National Bureau of Economic Research. http://www.nber.org/papers/w18996.

Hidalgo, A. and R. Hausmann. 2009. The Building Blocks of Economic Complexity. *Proceedings of the National Academy of Sciences of the United States of America*. 106 (26). pp. 10570–10575.

Hidalgo, A. et al. 2007. The Product Space Conditions the Development of Nations. *Science* 317. pp. 482–487.

Hill, H. and J. Menon. 2011. Reducing Vulnerability in Transition Economies: Crises and Adjustment in Cambodia. *ASEAN Economic Bulletin*. 28 (2). pp. 134–59.

———. 2014. Cambodia: Rapid Growth in a Small, Open, Fragile, Post-Conflict Economy: Cambodia. *ADB Working Paper Series on Regional Economic Integration*. No. 141. https://www.adb.org/sites/default/files/publication/111031/reiwp-141-trade-policy-challenges-cambodia.pdf.

International Monetary Fund (IMF). 2021. 2021 *Article IV Consultation—Press Release and Staff Report*. https://www.imf.org/-/media/Files/Publications/CR/2021/English/1KHMEA2021002.ashx.

———. 2022. *Cambodia: 2022 Article IV Consultation—Press Release; Staff Report; and Statement by the Executive Director for Cambodia*. https://www.imf.org/en/Publications/CR/Issues/2022/12/15/Cambodia-2022-Article-IV-Consultation-Press-Release-Staff-Report-and-Statement-by-the-526993.

Kaldor, N. 1967. *Strategic Factors in Economic Development*. Cornell University.

Karamba, W., K. Tong, and I. Salcher. 2022. *Cambodia Poverty Assessment: Toward a More Inclusive and Resilient Cambodia*. World Bank. http://hdl.handle.net/10986/38344.

Kunmakara, M. 2023. NBC Pushes for De-dollarisation on 43rd Riel Day. *Phnom Penh Post*. 20 March. https://www.phnompenhpost.com/business/nbc-pushes-de-dollarisation-43rd-riel-day.

Kuznets, S. 1971. *Modern Economic Growth: Findings and Reflections.* Nobel Memorial Lecture, 11 December. https://www.nobelprize.org/prizes/economic-sciences/1971/kuznets/lecture/.

Lao-Arraya, K. 2002. How Can Cambodia, Lao PDR, Myanmar, and Viet Nam Cope with Revenue Lost due to AFTA Tariff Reductions. *ERD Working Paper Series.* No. 29. ADB. https://www.adb.org/sites/default/files/publication/28323/wp029.pdf.

Manyika, J. et al. 2017. *Jobs Lost, Jobs Gained: What the Future of Work Will Mean for Jobs, Skills, and Wages.* McKinsey Global Institute. https://www.mckinsey.com/featured-insights/future-of-work/jobs-lost-jobs-gained-what-the-future-of-work-will-mean-for-jobs-skills-and-wages.

Menon, J. 2008. Cambodia's Persistent Dollarization: Causes and Policy Options. *ASEAN Economic Bulletin.* 25 (2). pp. 228–237.

———. 2019. *Why the Fourth Industrial Revolution Could Spell More Jobs—Not Fewer.* World Economic Forum. https://www.weforum.org/agenda/2019/09/fourth-industrial-revolution-jobs/.

———. 2020. COVID-19 and the Poor. *Economics Working Paper* 2020-07. ISEAS-Yusof Ishak Institute. ISEAS_EWP_2020-7_Menon.pdf.

———. 2022a. ASEAN's Newer Members in Two Crises: Impact, Response, and Lessons. In H.E. Khor, D. Guinigundo, and M. Kawai, eds. *Trauma to Triumph: Rising from the Ashes of the Asian Financial Crisis.* AMRO. pp. 489–526. ISEAS_EWP_2022-1_Menon.pdf.

———. 2022b. The CLMV Countries and RCEP: Will They Grasp the Opportunities? *Fulcrum.* 18 February. https://fulcrum.sg/the-clmv-countries-and-rcep-will-they-grasp-the-opportunities/.

Menon, J. and V. Roth, eds. 2022. *Agricultural Trade between China and the Greater Mekong Subregion Countries: A Value Chain Analysis*. ISEAS-Yusof Ishak Institute.

National Institute of Statistics. various years. Cambodia Socio-Economic Survey.

Ngin, C. 2022. The Undetermined Costs and Benefits of Cambodia's Engagement with China's Belt and Road Initiative. *Perspective.* 2022/84. ISEAS-Yusof Ishak Institute. https://www.iseas.edu.sg/wp-content/uploads/2022/07/ISEAS_Perspective_2022_84.pdf.

Nuesch, S. 2007. *The Economics of Superstars and Celebrities.* Springer.

Organisation for Economic Co-operation and Development (OECD). 2016. *Automation and Independent Work in a Digital Economy: Policy Brief on the Future of Work*.

Santos, B. 2022. Cambodia's Steeplechase Towards Renewable Energy. *PV Magazine.* https://www.pv-magazine.com/2022/09/20/cambodias-steeplechase-towards-renewable-energy/.

Sustainable Development Report: Cambodia. Citing Sachs, J. D., G. Lafortune, and G. Fuller. 2024. *The SDGs and the UN Summit of the Future. Sustainable Development Report 2024.* SDSN and Dublin University Press. https://dashboards.sdgindex.org/profiles/cambodia.

United Nations (UN), ADB, and United Nations Development Programme (UNDP). 2023. *Delivering on the Sustainable Development Goals through Solutions at the Energy, Food and Finance Nexus*. United Nations. http://dx.doi.org/10.22617/TCS230094-2.

United Nations Capital Development Fund (UNCDF). 2021. *Cambodia Financial Inclusion Refresh*. https://www.uncdf.org/Download/AdminFileWithFilename?id=16788&cultureId=127&filename=4-4-2022map-diagnostic-refresh-for-cambodiapdf.

UNDP. 2019. *Cambodia: Derisking Renewable Energy Investment*. https://www.undp.org/sites/g/files/zskgke326/files/2022-09/DREI%20Cambodia%20Full%20Report%20%28English%29%20%28Jun%202019%29%20%28FINAL%29.pdf.

Warr, P. and J. Menon. 2016. Cambodia's Special Economic Zones. *ADB Economic Working Paper Series*. No. 459. pp. 273–290. https://www.adb.org/sites/default/files/publication/175236/ewp-459.pdf.

World Bank. 2021. *The State of the Global Education Crisis: A Path to Recovery*.

———. 2022. *Cambodia Economic Update: Navigating Global Economic Headwinds*. https://documents.worldbank.org/en/publication/documents-reports/documentdetail/099240011302241362/p17734004eeaaf0ee08c1e01df07b5a22df.

World Travel and Tourism Council. 2018. *Cambodia Economic Impact Report*. Oxford Economics.

www.ingramcontent.com/pod-product-compliance
Lightning Source LLC
Chambersburg PA
CBHW041758220926
51847CB00014B/242
* 9 7 8 9 2 9 2 7 0 9 7 1 6 *